# WITHDRAWN

# MEAT and POTATOES

MARGARET MORGAN
and
MARY MORGAN PEDLOW

Memorial

RIVERSIDE PUBLIC LIBRARY

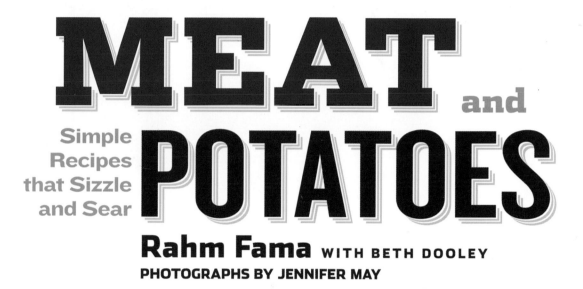

# MEAT and POTATOES

## Simple Recipes that Sizzle and Sear

**Rahm Fama** WITH BETH DOOLEY

PHOTOGRAPHS BY JENNIFER MAY

CLARKSON POTTER/PUBLISHERS
NEW YORK

Copyright © 2014 by Rahm Fama
Photographs copyright © 2014 by Jennifer May

All rights reserved.
Published in the United States by Clarkson Potter/Publishers,
an imprint of the Crown Publishing Group, a division of Random
House LLC, a Penguin Random House Company, New York.
www.crownpublishing.com
www.clarksonpotter.com

CLARKSON POTTER is a trademark and POTTER with colophon is
a registered trademark of Random House LLC.

Library of Congress Cataloging-in-Publication Data
Fama, Rahm.
   Meat and potatoes : simple recipes that sizzle and sear /
Rahm Fama with Beth Dooley ; photographs
by Jennifer May. —First edition.
     pages cm
Includes index.
1. Cooking (Meat) 2. Cooking (Vegetables) 3. Quick and easy
cooking. I. Dooley, Beth. II. Title.
TX749.F27 2014
641.6'6—dc23                              2013013583

ISBN 978-0-307-98524-8
eBook ISBN 978-0-307-98525-5

Printed in China

Book and cover design by Ashley Tucker
Book and cover photography by Jennifer May

10  9  8  7  6  5  4  3  2  1

First Edition

I dedicate this book to every cook who put in all those long hours with me to make that dinner rush possible. I could never have done it without you.

CONT

ENTS

This book was inspired by my desire to share what I've learned as a rancher, chef, dad, and host of my TV show, *Meat & Potatoes*. I have combed the country for the choicest cuts of beef, pork, lamb, and poultry. Along with fellow chefs, foodies, and chowhounds, I've obsessed over local fare from New York to San Francisco, Chicago to Austin, and cities and towns in between. I've devoted my career to meat—how it's raised and processed, where to find the best, how to prepare it, and how to create beautiful accompaniments for full, satisfying plates.

I grew up on my mom's cattle ranch outside Santa Fe, New Mexico, near my extended family of grandparents, aunts, uncles, and cousins. Living on a ranch, I worked all the time. It was just expected. My favorite chore was to help the ranch hands move steers through the grassy foothills under the big and bright western sky. Some nights I'd join in their dinners of steaks and chiles grilled over an open fire.

Every morning, my grandmother rose early to make tortillas that she'd cook on a big cast-iron skillet that she kept right on the stove all the time. In fact, she cooked just about everything on that skillet, which seemed ever ready to sear pork for chili or beef for carnitas. My grandmother's tortillas were thick and chewy, more like naan bread than thin, flat tortillas, and they lasted us through the day. For big family meals, I'd often help my grandmother make pozole, which is a classic Southwestern stew made of hominy (traditional dried corn that's been reconstituted into plump, soft kernels) and pork; tamales with fresh masa (corn flour) wrapped and steamed in corn husks; and carne adovada with red chiles and pork. On nights when I came home late, my grandfather would rise to meet me. He'd make a fresh pot of coffee and we'd warm up the leftover tortillas in the big cast-iron skillet and slather them with peanut butter and jelly for a snack. Then we'd sit back to chat well into the wee hours. Early in the morning, I'd wake to the sound of my grandmother making black beans or chili con carne using an old pressure cooker. This big deep stew pot had a lid with a metal temperature gauge that rattled on top as the contents bubbled away and finished cooking.

We also raised sheep for my grandfather and when I turned nine years old, I was considered grown up enough to help him with the slaughter. On birthdays and holidays my grandparents would gather all the relatives and their friends to roast lamb in the huge brick fire pit near the adobe home that my grandfather, a mason, built himself. As

Here I'm mixing up the ingredients on my mom's "feed-truck." When I wasn't cooking for people, I was serving up meals for the cattle.

we basted the lamb with a chili sauce, its juices would spit and hiss on the coals. My grandparents and mom used every part of the animals we raised, from the snout to the hooves, and whatever was left, we'd craft into a tasty soup. We wasted nothing.

My grandmother also made our beef jerky from scratch. She'd marinate a beef roast and rub it with dried chile pepper, freeze it, then have Johnny's Market Butcher, which was not far from her house, slice it into strips so thin they were nearly transparent enough to read a newspaper through them. Using a wooden clothespin, she'd clip each strip to the clothesline running down the hall from the kitchen to my bedroom. Every night when I went to bed, I'd take a good bite out of each slice as it was drying. One year, I ate at least half the batch before it was dry and finished.

My favorite time of year was October, when the New Mexico chile peppers were trucked in from the farms in the Hatch Canyon area, 250 miles south of Santa Fe and near the Mexican border. These peppers, irrigated with the nutrient-rich red clay of the Rio Grande, are distinctly dense and spicy. The local grocery stores set out enormous roasters that filled Santa Fe with sweet-spicy smoke. We'd lug home burlap sacks of fresh peppers to roast in our fire pit. My grandmother blackened them over the flames, I was the peeler, and my mother fit them into zip-lock plastic bags. Inevitably, I'd rub my eyes or scratch my arm, and I'd sting and burn for hours.

Santa Fe has always been a great food town, where outside every café and diner there's a smoker fashioned out of an old oil drum for barbecue pork and beef. Ancho chiles hang to dry on shop walls and hot sauce, not ketchup, is served with fries. By the time I was in high school, Southwestern cuisine had captured the nation's attention. Most of my friends' families worked in the rapidly growing restaurant industry and they all loved to cook at home, too. In their kitchens I was introduced to fresh foods I'd never tasted before—asparagus, artichokes, snap peas, baby greens, lots of fresh herbs. These brought a new dimension to the

> By the time I was in high school, Southwestern cuisine had captured the nation's attention.

familiar dinners of beans and rice, pork and beef seared in the skillet, and the tortillas and tamales I ate at home. Whenever I was invited for dinner at a friend's house, I'd hang out in the kitchen, ask questions, and help cook.

My first "real" job in high school was at Mark Miller's Coyote Café, where I bussed tables and cleaned floors. The casual and friendly restaurant served regional specialties made from scratch, such as chicken mole, tomatillo salsa, quesadillas, refried beans, and tamales, all made with local ingredients. This professional kitchen fascinated me. The mix of sizzling steaks and roasting peppers, the cooks' laughter and jokes, and the fast pace of the place drew me inside. What really amazed me was how each cook managed his station and produced a plate to serve so quickly. I probably made a pest out of myself, but eventually the chef promoted me to prep cook. I took on as many shifts as I could—so many that I focused on learning to cook instead of studying for my classes. I hauled crates of potatoes (and peeled hundreds of them all morning). I filleted fish, and I removed silverskin from beef. Pretty soon I moved up to sauté cook and learned to turn out perfectly fried potatoes and polenta in minutes, right in sync with the grill guy.

# By my senior year in high school, I knew this was the career for me. I would be a chef.

From the open kitchen, I could look out into the dining room and see how my food was received. I loved watching people laugh and chat, sharing dishes, and enjoying each other's company over the plates I'd prepared. I'd hear snatches of comments and compliments, and leave my shift, well past midnight, feeling encouraged. While my high school friends played on the football team and went to parties, I raced back to my station, took on more kitchen tasks, and welcomed new challenges. By my senior year in high school, I knew this was the career for me. I would be a chef.

I didn't have the funds for a culinary institute, so I enrolled in the school of hard knocks. With $49 in my pocket, I rode a bus to Austin, Texas, where I'd been invited to help a friend of my former boss open a new restaurant, the West Bank Fish Camp, on the shores of Lake Austin. By my twenty-fifth birthday, I'd cooked at Quail Run in Santa Fe,

Phoenician in Scottsdale, and Broadmoor Hotel in Colorado Springs. Those experiences elevated me to executive chef at the acclaimed Raoul's in New York City. Serge Raoul handed me full creative license in his family's SoHo bistro, known for its authentic and eclectic casual fare. Next, I took over the kitchens of various Rock Resorts: La Posada de Santa Fe Resort and Spa and the Wildflower at the Lodge, in Vail.

I am a curious cook, eager to learn about new ingredients and techniques that I can use both at home and in my restaurant kitchens. I practiced the art of Argentinean grilling while living in a cabin in the Colorado mountains outside Vail. The six-foot-tall fireplace there was perfect for roasting big cuts of meat and vegetables and for grilling steaks. I'd also bake cornbread in a cast-iron skillet set over the coals, piling embers on its lid as a makeshift oven. The cornbread would emerge with a fine, firm crust and tender center. While it's been a true honor to cook in some of the best kitchens in the country, including the James Beard House in New York City, my favorite meals are the ones I've created for family and friends using the simplest equipment to make the foods I grew up with and still love. For me, nothing is more fun than drawing friends into the kitchen, giving each one an assignment, and pulling together a wonderful meal.

The keys to my cooking are top-notch ingredients from local sources—they have the best flavor so that all I really need to do as a chef is to cook them quickly and simply. I find them from ranchers and farmers who raise their animals the way my family did—with respect. I get to know the people who supply my food and I make time to visit their ranches and farms. After years of living in different areas of the country, working in a variety of kitchens, I have settled in Southern California, near Los Angeles, and have enjoyed getting to know the area through its restaurants, producers, and farmers. I often travel the country introducing chefs to new products and equipment and teaching them new techniques. Being home in the kitchen with my kids and my friends is my way of winding down. The first thing I do when I walk in the door after a long day is to grab my cast-iron skillet and start pulling ingredients out of cupboards and the refrigerator. In just minutes, the wonderful smells coming from the kitchen draw my kids in, and pretty soon we're chatting and talking as they help me cook.

My childhood experiences raising animals and then partaking in their slaughter provided me the best lessons any chef can have. This food is precious and I treat it with care. Though my kids are not with me full time, whenever we are together, we cook at home as much as possible. Both my son and daughter love my stories about the ranches our meat comes from and how it got to our plates. They accompany me to various farms and ethnic grocery stores near L.A. to buy the ingredients for our meals. Like all kids, mine are curious and hungry. They like the thrill of sizzling butter in a cast-iron skillet and flipping a steak over flames on the grill. Though it's hard, even for me, to compete with the bright packaging of convenience foods, I've found that when I can get my kids to help cook, they will eat what we make at home. We save bones from chickens to make stock, leftover steak is used for sandwiches, and we collect the bacon grease in a coffee can, just as my grandmother once did. There's no better fat for pan-roasting beef tenderloin.

**Checking to be sure the cattle are healthy on my mom's cattle ranch, Santa Fe.**

I have organized this book so each menu includes recipes for a meat dish plus two suggested sides, one starch and one vegetable. My recipes are straightforward and uncomplicated, as well as flavorful and fun. They were created to engage friends and families who may want to join in preparing simple, delicious meals. The quantities are for six people, enough to feed a family and maybe have leftovers for the sandwiches that conclude each chapter. At the back of the book I've also included a chapter of one-pot recipes that create new dishes from a previous dinner. If you're short on time, don't worry about making every recipe for each meal. You can always just make the meat dish, then add a tossed salad and crusty bread. In some cases, you may find that two side dishes add up to a delicious vegetarian entrée. And have fun mixing and matching! Enjoy!

# BUYING YOUR MEAT

Today, there are more options than ever before for buying quality meat. I suggest creating relationships with the people you buy your meat from. Don't hesitate to ask questions about the sourcing and how the animals were raised. Good butchers, meat department grocery managers, and farmers like to share what they know. It's better to pay a little more for good quality from someone you trust. As more home cooks become interested in buying local foods, the markets have expanded to meet the demand. Here are several ways to buy your meat:

- Supermarkets may offer the lowest prices, but the quality can be inconsistent. To be sure you're buying the best, check the "What to Look For" section that follows. Some stores will custom-cut meat upon request.

- A local butcher shop is a valuable source of good meat and information. Most butchers have a relationship with local farms and can tell you where and how an animal was raised as well as how to handle and cook the meat.

- Farmers' markets are a great place to meet local farmers and ranchers who sell free-range and grass-fed meat. Don't hesitate to ask questions. You'll learn a great deal.

- Community-supported agriculture (CSA) is an arrangement in which individuals pay in advance for a year's share of meat (and often other farm products), then pick up the weekly share from the farm or a drop-off site. It's a program used by small vegetable farmers that is now being extended to ranchers and dairy farmers.

- Buying a whole animal directly from a farm provides individuals with a direct source for meat. In this arrangement the farm sells a whole animal to an individual or a group and has it slaughtered and then butchered into cuts. This is an economical way to source good-quality local meat.

## WHAT TO LOOK FOR

When selecting meat, I rely on my ability to judge a good cut, but it's not always possible to inspect the meat directly. Labels at the supermarket offer some clues to quality. The most familiar terms for high-quality meat are "certified organic" and "natural," which are regulated and defined by the United States Department of Agriculture (USDA). "Natural" means the meat has been minimally processed and contains no artificial flavors, colors, or preservatives. "Certified organic" indicates that the animal was raised on feed that was 100 percent organically grown and was not given antibiotics or hormones. These terms do not indicate whether or not the animal was raised humanely.

"Grass-fed," "pastured," or "free range" are the terms I look for. They indicate that the animal has grazed freely outside. It's the most

**Hungry cattle waiting for that special feed my mom mixed.**

humane way to raise animals, and the meat is lower in fat and calories and higher in omega-3 fatty acids. Grass-fed animals are naturally healthy and so do not need to be treated with antibiotics. For beef and lamb, the best is free-range, then corn-finished or grain-finished just before slaughter. This allows the animals to develop a little extra fat for flavor and texture.

It is really up to you, the consumer, to decide how important organic, grass-fed, and free-range meat is to you and your family. I consider free-range more important than organic. Though free-range is more expensive than conventional meat, free-range costs less than organic.

Whether you are buying your meat from the grocery store or the back of a farmer's van, you'll want to recognize a good-quality piece of meat. Here are a few guidelines:

- Different cuts deserve different treatments. An expensive piece of beef tenderloin will make a terrible stew, while an inexpensive shoulder doesn't work on the grill. Therefore, shopping by price isn't necessarily the way to go. Throughout these pages, I specify the best cooking techniques for the various cuts. But if you're not sure, ask the butcher.

- If the meat is already packaged, pay attention to the "sell-by" date. Do not buy meat beyond its "sell-by" date.

- Good meat is firm. If packaged, it should be springy and not sag under the wrap.

- The fat can tell you a great deal; it should be as firm as hard butter, not mushy. It should cut straight through with a little resistance and the knife should come out clean, not streaked with a lot of grease.

- The color of beef should be cherry red, not bright pink or brown. Lamb should be light red; pork and veal should be rosy pink; chicken should never be slimy or have a greenish cast.

- Meat should not have an odor. If there is any scent at all, it should be slightly metallic.

Once you've purchased your meat, store it safely. Here are some tips:

- You want the meat to stay moist without becoming wet and sticky; it should be a little dry on the surface, but not dried out. If the meat is wrapped in plastic, unwrap it and rinse under cold water, then pat dry with paper towels. Wrap it in parchment or butcher paper, then put it in a resealable plastic bag and keep it in the back of the refrigerator, where it's coldest. Plastic traps moisture, making the meat wet and soggy, but if it's left unwrapped, it will dry out. The parchment protects the meat, allows the airflow, and keeps it from becoming too soggy.

- Use the meat within five days or freeze it (details follow).

- I prefer to freeze large cuts and whole birds (chickens, turkeys, ducks) rather than cutting and freezing smaller portion sizes. Meat tends to dry out when it's frozen, so the less surface area that is exposed in the freezer, the moister and juicier the meat will be once thawed. Larger cuts freeze better than smaller ones because they retain moisture; smaller cuts dry out over time.

- To freeze meat, follow the directions for storing meat in a resealable plastic bag, then store it in the freezer for up to six months. Be sure to label and date the packages.

- Thaw frozen meat in the refrigerator slowly; this may take up to two days depending on the size of the cut. In a restaurant kitchen, this slow thawing process is called "slacking." When meat thaws too rapidly, the tissues break down, destroying the juices and flavor, meaning that texture and taste will be compromised. Never thaw meat in the microwave or under hot running water.

- Once thawed, cook the meat within one day.

# TWO KITCHEN ESSENTIALS FOR COOKING MEAT

## THE ESSENTIAL CAST-IRON SKILLET

The most important piece of equipment in my kitchen is the cast-iron skillet. Look for this icon noting recipes where I recommend its use. It distributes the heat evenly and, when properly seasoned, keeps the meat from sticking to it better than any nonstick pan.

If you purchase a new cast-iron skillet, season it before using. Rub a thin coat of vegetable oil, shortening, or lard into the pan with a paper towel or cotton cloth until it looks as if there's no oil left on the surface. Place the pan upside down on a baking sheet in a 450°F oven for thirty minutes. Turn off the heat and let the pan cool in the oven. Repeat four times in a row before using the pan for the first time. When seasoned, it's ready to use. To clean a seasoned pan after cooking, simply wipe it well with a damp paper towel or dishrag. Do not use soap and do not soak the pan, as this would ruin the seasoning. If it needs scrubbing, use coarse salt to remove any crusts of food, then wipe it clean with a damp towel. The more you cook with a seasoned pan, the stronger the seasoning will be.

## THERMOMETERS

Even though I've been cooking meat for about thirty years, I still rely on a thermometer when cooking at home. It will ensure success. Throughout the book you'll find more complete explanations of various cooking methods, along with the different temperatures that indicate when the meat is done. Here are the kinds of meat thermometers on the market; some are quite simple, others more elaborate. Whatever you buy, make a commitment to use it.

- **STANDARD DIAL THERMOMETER:** This is the most basic mercury thermometer; it's simply a dial attached to a stem with a sharp metal point that's inserted into the meat. These are easy to use and virtually indestructible. Most are heatproof so they can cook along with the meat (make sure yours is oven safe so you don't melt it!).

- **DIGITAL INSTANT-READ THERMOMETER:** Ranging from simple digital thermometers to large fancy gadgets with timers and alarms, these require batteries and most are not heatproof. Some special grilling and fireplace forks have built-in digital thermometers so you can test the doneness of your meat without burning yourself.

- **WIRELESS MEAT THERMOMETER:** Here, a heat-sensitive probe inserted into the meat is connected by a heatproof wire to a digital transmitter. This allows you to track the meat's temperature from afar, so you can enjoy a drink in the living room with your friends and still monitor the meat. It also eliminates the need to constantly lift the grill hood or open the oven (which lowers the cooking temperature and throws off the timing). Some have alarms that alert you to doneness.

- **POP-UP THERMOMETER:** Used on turkeys and chicken, this is not really a thermometer but a plastic or metal stem that is stuck into the fowl's breast; when the internal temperature reaches the desired number, a plug pops up to indicate doneness. These are not accurate and are not reusable.

## GENERAL GUIDELINES FOR COOKING MEAT

- Always bring the meat to room temperature before cooking. All of the recipes in this book have been calibrated to begin with the meat at room temperature. Cold meat will take longer to cook and will cook unevenly.

- Be sure to remove every bit of silverskin, the shiny coating that covers some pieces of meat, before cooking. Use a sharp paring knife or ask the butcher to do it for you.

- Season the meat on all sides with freshly ground black pepper and a little salt.

- To ensure the meat cooks to the recommended temperature, use a meat thermometer.

- After the meat is cooked, allow it to rest so the juices redistribute as the meat cools. Resting is essential for a flavorful, juicy piece of meat.

- Look for this icon noting less-than-one-hour recipes.

# BEEF

My mom cares deeply about the cattle on her ranch. A strong and gentle woman, she helped us understand the important role these animals played in our lives as a source of food and income for our entire family. "We must keep them happy and healthy," she constantly reminded me when I was growing up. So, just as the son of a fisherman from Nantucket would have a great appreciation for the fish he catches, I have tremendous respect for cattle and an intuitive understanding of meat. I know how much the care with which an animal is raised, the pasture, and the diet affect the flavor and texture of any cut. Every good chef understands this. My focus when cooking beef is on working with its natural flavor and cooking properties, so I keep things simple.

While it's important to understand the different grades of beef as defined below, you should learn to use your own sense of touch and smell to determine beef's quality. The best beef is firm and bright red, with a fine sheen of fat that resembles candle wax. When properly aged, it will have a slightly musty smell. Lower grades are limp, slightly mushy, and watery and have no distinct smell.

## SELECTING BEEF

The United States Department of Agriculture (USDA) uses eight grades, but here is what you need to know:

**PRIME** grade, the highest, is cut from young cattle and has the most marbling, so it's juicy and flavorful. Prime cuts are excellent for dry-heat cooking such as grilling.

**CHOICE** grade has less marbling than prime but is the most popular grade because it's tasty, tender, and affordable. Most cuts work well for dry-heat cooking.

**SELECT** grade is especially lean because it has the least marbling. It's better suited to low, slow, moist heat.

Take these factors into consideration when selecting beef:

Pastured and grass-fed animals raised outside produce the leanest beef. When pastured cattle are fed a diet of grain just before slaughter, they develop some fat and marbling. The best-tasting beef comes from cattle that are grass-fed and grain-finished. This is not always a term used on package labels, but it is noted in good butcher shops and at farmers' markets.

Aging improves the flavor and texture of beef, infusing it with a buttery character and deeper beef taste. Most steaks have been wet-aged, a process that seals the meat in a vacuum pack and refrigerates it. Purists will argue that dry-aging beef by storing it unwrapped in a controlled environment for several weeks will concentrate its flavor. Dry-aged beef is higher in price, but once you taste it, you'll understand why.

# GENERAL RULES FOR COOKING BEEF

- After you remove the beef from the refrigerator, season it with salt and pepper, then place it on a rack over a platter or rimmed baking sheet. The tray will catch any blood and the rack will allow the air to circulate and help keep the meat dry. The drier the surface of the meat, the better it will sear.

- Most people like their beef cooked to medium, 135°F. Once you've mastered this standard, you can gauge whether you prefer your beef cooked slightly more for medium-well or less for medium-rare.

- To test the temperature of the meat, insert the instant-read thermometer into the meat closest to the bone, which tends to cook a little more slowly than the edges of a cut.

- When the meat is done, set it on a rack over a platter or rimmed baking sheet. This allows the flavorful juices that have been drawn to the surface by heat to be reabsorbed and retained by the meat before it's sliced. (By resting the meat on a rack, you keep the juices from being pressed out under the weight of the cut.)

# CUTS OF BEEF

Here is a quick guide to matching the cut of beef to the appropriate cooking method.

**FRESH GROUND BEEF:** Used for hamburgers, meatballs, and skillet dishes, ground beef should be purchased with an eye toward the "sell-by" date on the package. Remember that color is not always an indication of freshness. Beef may appear bright red on the surface but if exposed to oxygen, it may turn brown. These changes are normal. When purchasing ground beef, know that the leaner it is, the more quickly it will cook and become dried out. Here's a guide to ground beef:

- Ground chuck comes from the shoulder of the cow. Its fat content varies between 15 and 20 percent. It has a rich flavor and is moist and tender, best for hamburgers.

- Ground sirloin, with 7 to 10 percent fat content, is cut from the middle of the animal. It can dry out quickly, so is best used in meat sauces.

- Ground round, from the rump, contains 20 percent fat and is rough or gristly; it's best for dishes where texture is not critical, such as Rahm's Childhood Corn Chip Pie (page 217).

- Ground beef is a term I suggest you avoid. This combines several cuts and the fat content can range as high as 30 percent, making it greasy.

**STEAKS:** The most tender steaks are cut from the center (rib and loin) of the animal. Premium steaks are strip (top loin), T-bone, porterhouse, rib eye, and tenderloin and are the most expensive. A little less tender, less expensive, yet full of flavor are top sirloin, flat iron, chuck eye, and round tip. These are best grilled or cooked quickly.

Steaks from the fore- and hindquarters are a little tougher, even less expensive, and full-flavored. These require marinades for grilling or moist, low heat. They include bottom round, chuck shoulder, and skirt steaks.

**OVEN ROASTS:** Roasts are thicker than two inches and are most often cooked in the oven or on a covered grill.

- Premium roasts include rib, top loin, and tenderloin. These are the most tender and most costly.

- Everyday roasts that are leaner and more economical include tri-tip, rump, and bottom round; these may be braised or roasted in the oven, partially covered. This is a cut often used for kebabs or stir-fries, too.

**POT ROASTS** are cut from the fore- and hindquarters, with more muscle and connective tissue. Moist, low-temperature cooking for these cuts is best. Chuck, rump, and brisket make the best pot roasts and braises. Cut a chuck or rump roast into cubes to make a flavorful stew.

# GRILLED T-BONE STEAK
## SWEET POTATO MASH
# KIMCHI

 A T-bone steak has a dual personality. The side closest to the bone is as juicy and delicate as a filet mignon, while the meat nearest the edge is as robust and flavorful as a good New York strip. This menu is my go-to on a busy night. My daughter likes to help smash the sweet potatoes with a potato masher and finish the last steps herself. T-bones have a rich beefy flavor that is the perfect foil to the fiery tang of kimchi. My shortcut version of this Korean relish yields the same vibrant flavors in far less time than traditional recipes. **SERVES 6**

## Grilled T-Bone Steak

**3 12-ounce T-bone steaks, 2 inches thick**

**Salt and freshly ground black pepper**

**1.** Prepare a gas or charcoal grill or preheat the broiler to high. Preheat the oven to 350°F, if cooking outdoors.

**2.** Pat the steaks dry, and season with salt and pepper.

**3.** Grill the steaks, turning the meat clockwise every 5 minutes, for a total of 10 minutes. Then flip the steaks and repeat, turning clockwise every 5 minutes, for 10 more minutes. (Alternatively, broil the steaks for 15 minutes on each side.)

**4.** Transfer the steaks to a rack set over a roasting pan and cook in the oven for 5 to 10 minutes, until a meat thermometer inserted near the bone reads 135°F. Remove the steaks, season both sides with salt and pepper, and set on a rack over a platter. Allow the meat to rest for 10 to 15 minutes before slicing the steaks.

> **TIP** Those diamond grill marks on a properly grilled steak-house steak indicate that the steak has been turned more than once on a side.

# Sweet Potato Mash

**5 medium sweet potatoes, peeled and cut into 2-inch chunks**

**1 cup chicken stock**

**1 tablespoon honey**

**Salt and freshly ground black pepper**

**1.** Put the potatoes into a medium pot with the stock, honey, and enough water to just cover. Set over high heat and bring to a boil. Reduce the heat so the liquid simmers, cover, and cook for 15 minutes, or until the potatoes are tender when sliced with a knife.

**2.** Remove the potatoes and strain the liquid into a large pitcher; return the potatoes to the pot. Using a potato masher, smash the potatoes, adding enough of the cooking liquid to create a thick mash, then season with salt and pepper.

TIP Be sure to use real sweet potatoes, not yams, in this recipe. Though they look alike, they're not at all related. Sweet potatoes have a much sweeter flavor and denser flesh than yams. Plus, they're higher in vitamins and nutrients.

# Kimchi

1 large head Napa (Chinese) cabbage

1 red onion

3 tablespoons olive oil

1 teaspoon dark sesame oil

2 tablespoons hot chili paste

⅓ cup rice wine vinegar

2 tablespoons soy sauce

2 bunches scallions, both white and green parts

Salt and freshly ground black pepper

**1.** Prepare a gas or charcoal grill or preheat the broiler to high.

**2.** Remove any loose and damaged leaves from the cabbage head. Cut the head lengthwise into quarters and remove some of the core, but leave the quarters intact. Cut the red onion horizontally into ¼-inch slices. Toss the cabbage and onion with just enough of the olive oil to lightly coat.

**3.** In a large bowl, whisk together the sesame oil, chili paste, vinegar, and soy sauce and set aside.

**4.** Grill the cabbage quarters and the red onion 2 minutes per side, just until they are nicely charred, being careful not to overcook. (Alternatively, place the cabbage and onion on a baking sheet or broiling pan and broil for 2 minutes per side.)

**5.** Cut the cabbage into 3-inch-wide strips with a sharp knife. Cut the scallions in half horizontally. Transfer the cabbage, onion, and scallions to the bowl and toss with the dressing. Season with salt and pepper.

# PAN-SEARED RIB-EYE STEAK
# PARSLEY NEW POTATOES
# GREEN CHILE MUSHROOMS

I featured this steak topped with the green chile mushrooms on Food Network's *The Best Thing I Ever Ate*. It's a hit with everyone who has enjoyed this meal. The key is to choose a certified USDA Prime rib-eye steak for optimum flavor. The fat in a prime cut makes all the difference. It should be white and generous. The cast-iron skillet also makes a big difference in getting a great crusty sear on the meat for this dish. Don't be afraid to use very high heat when cooking the steak; you may set off a fire alarm once in a while to get this dish right. High heat gives your meat a thick, crusty coating that leaves behind those nubs that make great pan sauce. The mushrooms are delicious served over the steak and potatoes. **SERVES 6**

## Pan-Seared Rib-Eye Steak

**6 12-ounce USDA Prime rib-eye steaks**

**Salt and freshly ground black pepper**

**1 to 2 tablespoons olive oil**

**1.** Pat the steaks dry, and season with salt and pepper.

**2.** Heat the oil in a cast-iron skillet or heavy sauté pan over high heat. Working in batches so as not to crowd the pan, sear the steaks, one or two at a time, for 8 to 10 minutes so they develop a good firm crust, then flip the steaks and sear for another 8 to 10 minutes.

**3.** Transfer the steaks to a rack set over a platter, season with salt and pepper, and let stand for at least 10 minutes before serving.

## Parsley New Potatoes

18 to 24 small red new potatoes (3 to 4 pounds)

1 teaspoon salt, plus more to taste

2 tablespoons chopped fresh flat-leaf parsley

1 tablespoon extra-virgin olive oil, or as needed

Freshly ground black pepper

**1.** Put the potatoes in a large pot with just enough water to cover and add the teaspoon of salt. Bring to a boil, reduce the heat, and simmer until the potatoes are soft but still firm, about 15 minutes.

**2.** Drain and transfer to a large bowl, then add the parsley and enough olive oil to lightly coat. Toss and season with salt and pepper.

## Green Chile Mushrooms

10 Anaheim chiles

¼ cup (½ stick) unsalted butter

1 pound button mushrooms, quartered

1 teaspoon chopped garlic

1 cup chicken stock

**1.** Use tongs to hold the chiles directly over the high flame of a gas burner or set them directly on a hot grill for 5 to 10 minutes. Turn them constantly, until they are roasted and blackened all around.

**2.** Drop the chiles into a plastic bag and allow them to cool. Peel off the skin, slice in half, and remove the seeds, being careful not to touch your eyes. Chop the chiles and place in a medium bowl.

**3.** In the cast-iron skillet the meat was cooked in or a medium skillet, melt the butter over medium-high heat and sauté the mushrooms until golden. Add the garlic and cook for 30 seconds, watching that it doesn't burn.

**4.** Whisk in the stock, then add the chiles and cook for 2 to 3 minutes, or until the liquid is reduced and the mixture is thick.

# PEPPER-CRUSTED NEW YORK STRIP STEAKS
# HAND-CUT FRIES
# WILTED MUSTARD GREENS

I perfected this recipe when working with Guy Raoul, the head chef at the esteemed Raoul's bistro in New York City. Be sure to use freshly crushed or coarsely ground pepper; it gives the steak a warm, aromatic kick and tenderizes the meat. The cast-iron skillet makes a big difference in giving the meat a good, thick crust. You can also cook the mustard greens in the skillet, just be careful not to overcook. **SERVES 6**

## Pepper-Crusted New York Strip Steaks

**6 12-ounce New York strip steaks**

**½ cup freshly crushed or coarsely ground black peppercorns**

**2 tablespoons unsalted butter**

**2 tablespoons olive oil**

**2 cups beef stock**

**1 cup brandy**

**1 cup heavy cream**

**Salt**

**1.** Pat the meat dry; the steaks should be slightly damp. Spread the pepper on a plate. Lay one side of each steak on the cracked pepper and press down hard so that the pepper clings to the meat. Set the peppered steaks on a rack set over a platter or rimmed baking sheet and bring to room temperature.

**2.** Set a cast-iron skillet or large heavy sauté pan over high heat. Add the butter and oil and cook for 1 minute, or until the butter turns a light brown (watch that it doesn't burn). Sear the peppered side of 1 or 2 steaks (do not crowd the pan) for 4 minutes, or until nicely browned. Flip and sear the other side. Transfer to a rack set over a baking sheet. Repeat with the remaining steaks.

**3.** Stir in the stock, scraping up the bits in the bottom of the pan, then the brandy and cream. Bring to a boil, reduce the heat, simmer for 5 to 7 minutes, or until the liquid is reduced to become thick enough to coat a spoon. Salt to taste and serve with the steaks.

# Hand-Cut Fries

**4 large russet potatoes**      **½ cup olive oil**      **Salt**

**1.** Prepare a large bowl of ice water.

**2.** Rinse and peel the potatoes and slice into ½-inch by 3-inch strips. Put the strips in the cold water for 3 to 4 minutes, then drain and pat dry. Let sit for 5 minutes.

**3.** In a large deep skillet, heat the oil over medium-high heat to 375°F. Working in batches, fry the potatoes for 5 to 10 minutes, until golden brown. Turn out onto paper towels and sprinkle with salt.


# Wilted Mustard Greens

**2 to 4 bunches mustard greens (1 to 1½ pounds)**      **1 tablespoon chopped garlic**      **Salt and freshly ground black pepper**

**2 tablespoons olive oil**

**1.** Rinse the greens and remove the tough stems, but keep the leaves intact.

**2.** Pour the oil into a cast-iron or large deep skillet and set over high heat until the oil shimmers. Add the garlic and the greens and toss once or twice, cooking for 15 to 30 seconds, until the greens are just wilted. Season with salt and pepper.

# 5-B BURGER
# SMOKED PAPRIKA PARSNIP FRIES
# ASPARAGUS WITH MINT HOLLANDAISE

This burger features my five favorite ingredients—beef, black pepper, bacon, blue cheese, and basil butter. I like to use a mix of chuck and short rib ground medium. A good butcher can create a custom blend for you. The best way to cook a burger is in a cast-iron skillet. A flat grill, or plancha, works well, too. You want to create a good hard sear that traps the juices and adds crunch. I coat the meat lightly with cracked pepper to add flavor and a little more texture. Make the patties thick, so they stay juicy. The oven-roasted paprika fries pack a smoky punch and are healthy and light. Bright green asparagus with a minty hollandaise adds an elegant note. **SERVES 6**

## 5-B Burger

3 pounds 85% lean ground chuck

3 tablespoons coarsely ground black pepper

12 ounces sliced bacon

3 tablespoons bacon fat or olive oil

12 ounces blue cheese

¾ cup (1½ sticks) unsalted butter, softened

3 ounces fresh basil, chopped

6 soft burger buns, toasted

**1.** Shape the meat into six 8-ounce patties. Spread the pepper on a plate. Lightly press both sides in the pepper to coat. Set aside.

**2.** In a large skillet, cook the bacon until it's crisp and the fat is rendered. Remove and drain on paper towels. Save 3 tablespoons of the rendered bacon fat for cooking the burgers.

**3.** Set a cast-iron skillet, plancha, or heavy frying pan over medium-high heat. Generously film with the bacon fat or oil. Cook the burgers for 4 to 5 minutes, then flip and cook 4 more minutes. Top with the blue cheese and cook another 1 to 2 minutes, or until the cheese melts and an instant-read thermometer reaches 135°F.

**4.** In a small bowl, beat the butter and basil. Spread it on both sides of each bun. Place each patty on a bun and top with the bacon.

BEEF

## Smoked Paprika Parsnip Fries

2 pounds parsnips, peeled

2 tablespoons olive oil

¼ cup mayonnaise

1 tablespoon smoked paprika

Pinch of cayenne

1 teaspoon sherry vinegar

Salt and freshly ground black pepper

**1.** Preheat the oven to 350°F.

**2.** Cut the parsnips into sticks 4 inches long and ½ inch wide. Toss them with the olive oil and spread out on a baking sheet so that none of the pieces touch. Roast for 10 to 15 minutes, turning occasionally, until the parsnips are tender.

**3.** In a small bowl, whisk together the mayonnaise, smoked paprika, cayenne, and sherry vinegar. Coat the parsnips with the mayonnaise and season with salt and pepper as they come hot from the oven.

TIP I sometimes serve these hot, smoky-sweet parsnip fries as an appetizer with a side of the mint hollandaise or a good mayonnaise for dipping.

# Asparagus with Mint Hollandaise

2½ to 3 pounds jumbo asparagus

3 egg yolks

2 tablespoons freshly squeezed lime juice, or more to taste

1 cup (2 sticks) unsalted butter, melted

¼ teaspoon Tabasco sauce

1 tablespoon chopped fresh mint

**1.** In a large pot of rapidly boiling water, blanch the asparagus for 3 minutes until dark green, then drain in a colander. Transfer to a platter and cover with a towel to keep warm.

**2.** Fill the bottom of a double boiler with water and bring to a boil over high heat. Reduce the heat so the water simmers.

**3.** Whisk together the egg yolks and lime juice and turn into the top of the double boiler, then set over the simmering water. Whisk continuously until the eggs form thick ribbons, about 3 to 4 minutes.

**4.** Remove the eggs from the heat and very slowly, a little bit at a time, whisk in the melted butter, being careful to fully incorporate each addition for 2 minutes.

**5.** When all the butter has been incorporated, whisk in the Tabasco and mint and serve the asparagus drizzled with the hollandaise.

# ROASTED PRIME RIB-EYE STEAK "MUSHROOM" POTATOES CHIMICHURRI GARLIC-THYME ROMANESCA

Who doesn't love a great prime rib roast? I created this recipe to combine all the rich flavor of a good rib eye with the ease of a prime rib. Searing the steaks in a cast-iron skillet before putting them in the oven seals in the flavor. Be sure to baste them frequently with the pan juices to keep the steaks moist and flavorful. Romanesca, a beautiful pale-green variety of cauliflower with conical florets, becomes slightly nutty-tasting when roasted. Cutting the potatoes into "mushrooms" is easy and makes for a fun presentation, but if you're running short on time, simply quarter them instead. The zesty chimichurri is a classic South American steak sauce I learned to make from the Argentinean cooks who worked with me in Colorado. It adds zip to the potatoes and the steaks. **SERVES 6**

## Roasted Prime Rib-Eye Steak

2 to 2½ pounds whole prime bone-in rib-eye steaks, 1½ to 2 inches thick

Salt and freshly ground black pepper

2 tablespoons olive oil

1 tablespoon unsalted butter

**1.** Pat the meat dry, season with salt and pepper, and bring to room temperature.

**2.** Preheat the oven to 350°F.

**3.** Set a cast-iron skillet or large sauté pan over high heat and heat the oil and butter until it shimmers. Sear the steaks, holding each down by the bone to rock it back and forth, for 5 minutes per side. This will ensure a good, hard sear and lock in the flavor.

**(continues)**

**4.** Set the steaks on a rack over a baking pan and roast for 10 to 20 minutes, basting frequently with the pan juices, until an instant-read thermometer registers between 120°F for rare and 135°F for medium-rare, depending on your preference.

**5.** Remove the meat, season with salt and pepper, and return to the rack to rest for 10 minutes. To serve the steak, cut between the meat and bone of each steak and cut each steak crosswise into slices about 1 inch thick.

## "Mushroom" Potatoes Chimichurri

| | | |
|---|---|---|
| 18 to 24 small Red Bliss potatoes (4 to 5 pounds) | ½ cup chopped fresh cilantro | 2 tablespoons chopped shallots |
| 1 tablespoon salt | 1 tablespoon chopped garlic | Generous pinch of red pepper flakes |
| ½ cup chopped fresh flat-leaf parsley | | ½ cup olive oil |

**1.** Insert a sharp, round, metal tube a half inch into each potato. Using a sharp knife, cut in half above the tube. Remove the potato plug from the tube and work it into the stem hole created by the metal plug. Using a sharp knife, slice small circles from the "cap" in a polka dot pattern.

**2.** Place the potatoes in a pot, cover with cold water, add the salt, and bring to a gentle simmer. Poach for 15 to 20 minutes, until a knife pierces easily. Drain in a colander, then transfer to a large bowl.

**3.** In a small bowl, whisk together the parsley, cilantro, garlic, shallots, red pepper flakes, and oil. Pour over the potatoes and turn gently to coat.

# Garlic-Thyme Romanesca

1 teaspoon sugar

6 Romanesca or 2 heads broccoli or cauliflower, broken into florets

2 tablespoons olive oil

1 garlic clove, smashed

2 sprigs fresh thyme

Salt and freshly ground pepper

**1.** Bring a large pot of water to a boil and add the sugar. Cook the Romanesca until just tender, about 8 minutes. Then drain. Alternatively, cook the broccoli or cauliflower florets for 3 to 5 minutes.

**2.** In a medium saucepan set over medium heat, heat the oil and sauté the garlic and thyme for 30 seconds. Toss in the Romanesca and cook for 5 minutes, or until they begin to brown. Remove the thyme sprigs and season with salt and pepper before serving.

TIP

Roasting the Romanesca (as well as other cruciferous vegetables, such as broccoli, cauliflower, and cabbage) helps to caramelize their edges for a richer, slightly sweeter flavor. This recipe is equally delicious warm or at room temperature.

# FILET MIGNON
## SAVORY BREAD PUDDING MUFFINS
## CRISPY BRUSSELS SPROUTS

The tenderloin is such a lean cut, it needs to be seared in a generous amount of butter, oil, or bacon fat to help it develop a flavorful, thick crust before it's finished in the oven. For this, I rely on my trusty cast-iron skillet. You may want to use the rendered bacon fat from the Savory Bread Pudding Muffins, as my grandmother once did. They are luxuriously rich, a winning toss-up of the four "B's"—bacon, butter, blue cheese, and basil. Fresh, bright Brussels sprouts balance this plate.

**SERVES 6**

## Filet Mignon

| | | |
|---|---|---|
| **6 7- to 8-ounce center-cut tenderloin filets** | **Salt and freshly ground black pepper** | **2 tablespoons unsalted butter** |
| | | **2 tablespoons olive oil** |

**1.** Preheat the oven to 350°F.

**2.** Pat the filets dry. Season with salt and pepper.

**3.** In a cast-iron skillet or heavy frying pan, melt the butter and oil together over high heat. Sear the fillets one or two at a time (do not crowd the pan) for 4 minutes on each side, or until very crisp.

**4.** Set the filets on a roasting rack set on a baking sheet and bake for 10 to 15 minutes, until an instant-read thermometer inserted into the center registers 125°F for medium-rare (be careful, this meat can overcook in no time).

**5.** Salt and pepper both sides of the steaks and let rest uncovered for 3 to 5 minutes.

# Savory Bread Pudding Muffins

1 baguette

2 tablespoons unsalted butter

1 pound bacon, chopped

4 ounces blue cheese, crumbled

2 tablespoons sliced fresh basil

2 cups beef stock

1 cup heavy cream

Salt and freshly ground black pepper

**1.** Preheat the oven to 350°F.

**2.** Cut the baguette into 1-inch cubes.

**3.** Set a cast-iron skillet or large frying pan over medium heat and melt the butter. Add the croutons and cook for about 10 minutes, stirring constantly, until they turn golden brown, then transfer to a big bowl.

**4.** Add the bacon to the pan, set it over medium-high heat, and cook for 5 to 10 minutes, until the fat is rendered and the bacon is crisp.

**5.** Add half the bacon pieces and rendered fat to the bowl containing the croutons.

**6.** Reserve the remaining bacon fat and bacon pieces to make the Crispy Brussels Sprouts or to sear the tenderloins (or for another use).

**7.** Add three-quarters of the blue cheese, reserving the remainder for topping, the basil, stock, and cream to the croutons and toss. Set aside to allow the croutons to absorb the liquid for 1 hour. Season with salt and pepper.

**8.** Lightly grease 6 muffin cups. Distribute the bread mixture among the muffin cups. Sprinkle the reserved blue cheese on the top. Bake for 20 minutes, or until a knife inserted in the center comes out clean.

# Crispy Brussels Sprouts

**1 pound Brussels sprouts**

**½ cup sugar**

**2 tablespoons rendered bacon fat or olive oil**

**½ pound cooked bacon (from the Savory Bread Pudding Muffins)**

**1 tablespoon sherry vinegar or balsamic vinegar**

**Salt and freshly ground black pepper**

**1.** Clean the Brussels sprouts and trim off the bottoms. Put the Brussels sprouts and the sugar in a large pot with water to cover and bring to a boil over high heat. Reduce the heat and simmer the Brussels sprouts for 2 to 3 minutes, or until they are just tender and bright green. Drain and pat dry.

**2.** In a medium skillet, heat the bacon fat or oil over medium heat. Toss in the Brussels sprouts, stir until coated, and cook for 3 minutes, or until a knife pierces them easily.

**3.** Remove and toss with the cooked bacon pieces. Season with the vinegar and salt and pepper right before serving.

# PASTRAMI FLANK STEAK
## POTATO PANCAKES
# GINGERED RED CABBAGE SLAW

This zesty dry rub of fragrant spices sparks and tenderizes the flank steak. I use prepared pickling spice, available in the spice section of most grocery stores; bay seasoning or shrimp boil spices work nicely, too. You can make your own seasoning by blending 1 teaspoon each of mustard seeds, whole cloves, coriander seeds, and red pepper flakes, a bay leaf, and a cinnamon stick in a blender or food processor. After you've rubbed this dry marinade into the meat, put the steak in resealable plastic bags or a deep baking dish and refrigerate overnight. Once the steak is cooked, slice it very thin. The side dishes are inspired by classic Jewish deli fare—hearty potato pancakes and tangy slaw. Leftover steak and slaw are great the next day served on crusty buns. **SERVES 6**

---

## Pastrami Flank Steak

| | | |
|---|---|---|
| 1 4-pound flank steak | 1 tablespoon cinnamon | 1 cup coarse or kosher salt |
| 2 ounces pickling spice | ½ cup packed brown sugar | 1 tablespoon cracked black pepper |

**1.** Pat the meat dry. Cut the steak in half horizontally.

**2.** In a medium bowl, whisk together the pickling spice, cinnamon, brown sugar, salt, and 1 cup water. Rub this into both pieces of steak and then put the steaks in resealable plastic bags. Seal and refrigerate at least 2 hours or overnight.

**3.** Prepare a gas or charcoal grill, or preheat the broiler to high.

**4.** Remove the meat from the bag. Do not wipe off the marinade. Grill or broil the meat for 4 minutes per side. The sugars will caramelize and burn, giving the steak a flavorful crust. Transfer the steak to a rack set over a baking pan and sprinkle the cracked black pepper over the meat. Allow to rest for 5 minutes before carving into thin slices to serve.

# Potato Pancakes

4 medium russet potatoes, peeled

1 tablespoon chopped fresh flat-leaf parsley

1 small white onion, shredded

4 eggs, beaten

Salt and freshly ground black pepper

¼ cup olive oil

**1.** Preheat the oven to 375°F. Lightly grease a baking sheet or line with parchment paper.

**2.** Shred the potatoes. In a large bowl, stir together the potatoes, parsley, onion, and eggs, and season with salt and pepper.

**3.** Film a cast-iron or other medium skillet with 2 tablespoons of the oil and set over medium-high heat.

**4.** Scoop out ½ cup of the potato mixture for each pancake and fry for about 3 minutes per side, until nicely browned. Set the browned pancakes on the prepared baking sheet and put in the oven. Repeat with the remaining batter, adding more oil if necessary.

**5.** Bake for 5 minutes, or until cooked through and crisped. Season with salt and pepper.

# Gingered Red Cabbage Slaw

2 teaspoons Dijon mustard

¼ cup apple cider vinegar

1 tablespoon packed brown sugar

⅓ cup olive oil

3 cups cored and coarsely grated red cabbage

2 tart apples (Granny Smith or Honey Crisp), cored and shredded

1 large carrot, shredded

1 medium red onion, shredded

¼ cup chopped crystallized ginger

Salt and freshly ground black pepper

½ cup chopped fresh flat-leaf parsley

**1.** In a large bowl, whisk together the mustard, vinegar, and sugar. Whisk in the oil. Toss in the cabbage, apples, carrot, onion, and ginger. Season with salt and pepper.

**2.** Cover and refrigerate for 30 minutes before serving to allow the flavors to marry, or refrigerate overnight.

**3.** Toss in the parsley just before serving.

# NEW MEXICO RED CHILE & COFFEE CRUST TRI-TIP
# CREAMY CORN–BLUE CHEESE POLENTA
# CARAMELIZED CIPOLLINI ONIONS

Tri-tip is often overlooked, but it's flavorful and inexpensive, and the favorite cut for this cowboy classic. Traditionally this steak would be cooked in a cast-iron skillet over an open campfire under the stars. For the spice mix, I prefer the New Mexico red chile powder for its intense heat and smoky flavor, but use one you like. It's important to cook the meat to medium—130°F, no more, no less—and to rest it to allow the juices to be reabsorbed into the meat. Recalling the dishes of my youth that were seasoned with "corn smut," a mushroom that grows on corn, I use blue cheese in polenta to give it an authentic Mexican kick. The cipollini onions are mild-tasting, easy, and showy. They're fine made a day ahead and reheated before serving. Serve the onions on top of the polenta with the meat arranged on top. **SERVES 6**

## New Mexico Red Chile & Coffee Crust Tri-Tip

½ cup New Mexico red chile powder

½ cup finely ground coffee

¼ cup brown sugar

1 tablespoon salt

½ teaspoon black pepper

3 pounds tri-tip roast

1 tablespoon olive oil

2 tablespoons unsalted butter

**1.** Toss together the chile powder, coffee, sugar, salt, and pepper.

**2.** Pat the meat dry. Massage the mixture into the meat. Put in a large resealable plastic bag and allow it to come to room temperature.

**3.** Preheat the oven to 300°F. Heat the oil with the butter in a cast-iron skillet or a large ovenproof frying pan set over high heat. When it shimmers, sear the meat well, 5 minutes per side. (It will look as though it's burned, but that's from the coffee.) Put the skillet in the oven to finish cooking the meat, 3 to 5 minutes. It should register 130°F on an instant-read thermometer.

**4.** Remove and set on a rack over a platter or baking sheet and let rest for 15 to 30 minutes. Then carve against the grain.

# Creamy Corn–Blue Cheese Polenta

2 tablespoons unsalted
butter

1 small white onion,
chopped

6 cups whole milk

1 13-ounce package
instant polenta

4 ounces blue cheese

2 cups corn kernels,
fresh or frozen, thawed

Salt and freshly ground
black pepper

¼ cup diced scallions, both
white and green parts,
for garnish

**1.** Melt the butter in a large, deep saucepan over medium heat and
sauté the onion for 8 to 10 minutes, until light brown.

**2.** Using a wooden spoon, stir in the milk. Bring to a simmer
and gradually add the polenta in a slow, steady stream, stirring
constantly. Continue cooking and stirring the polenta for 2 to
3 minutes, or until it reaches the texture of a thick porridge.

**3.** Fold in the blue cheese and corn. Season with salt and pepper.
Serve garnished with the scallions.

# Caramelized Cipollini Onions

1 tablespoon unsalted
butter

18 to 24 pearl onions
(about 1½ pounds), peeled

1 sprig fresh rosemary

2 cups chicken stock

Salt and freshly ground
black pepper

**1.** In a cast-iron skillet set over medium heat, melt the butter.

**2.** Sauté the onions and rosemary for 8 to 10 minutes, until the
onions become a rich caramel-brown. Add enough stock to cover the
onions and the rosemary, and simmer until the liquid is reduced by
half. Remove the rosemary sprig.

**3.** Season to taste with salt and pepper. Spoon the onions with
their sauce over the polenta to serve.

MEAT AND POTATOES

# SHORT RIBS WITH LEMON AND THYME
# ROSEMARY BABY BLISS POTATOES
# ROASTED ARTICHOKE HEARTS

Start these ribs by searing them in a cast-iron skillet to create a crust and seal in flavor. Roast them for a long time until they are so tender they fall from the bone. You'll be rewarded by your patience, so just let them do their thing in the oven. Artichoke hearts, onion, garlic, and Red Bliss potatoes roast alongside, absorbing the juices, to provide a succulent, one-dish meal, finished with a final flourish—a sprinkling of lemon zest and salt. This is one of those dinners for a chilly winter's day—it steams the windows and fills your home with luxurious aromas. By the time it's ready, you will be starved and excited to dig in. **SERVES 6**

## Short Ribs with Lemon and Thyme

6 pounds beef short ribs

2 tablespoons olive oil

Freshly ground black pepper

1 tablespoon coarse or kosher salt

Grated zest and juice of 2 lemons

1 tablespoon fresh thyme leaves

**1.** Preheat the oven to 250°F.

**2.** Pat the meat dry, drizzle with the olive oil, and season with pepper.

**3.** Sear the ribs in a cast-iron skillet over high heat for 5 minutes per side, or until they've developed a firm crust.

**4.** Put the skillet in the oven and roast for 3 hours. Check halfway through—they should still look pale and gray; if the ribs are becoming dark, reduce the heat to 200°F. After 3 hours they should be crusty brown and very tender. If not, cook for another 15 minutes.

**5.** Put the salt in a nonstick skillet and set over medium-high heat. Stir in the lemon zest and thyme and toss together for 2 minutes so the salt absorbs the flavor.

**6.** Drizzle the lemon juice over the ribs and then sprinkle the salt mixture over the ribs and turn to coat. Allow the ribs to rest in the pan for 15 minutes before serving.

BEEF

## Rosemary Baby Bliss Potatoes

12 to 18 whole
baby bliss potatoes

1 white onion, sliced
½ inch thick

2 garlic cloves

4 sprigs fresh rosemary

1 tablespoon olive oil

Salt and freshly ground
black pepper

1. Preheat the oven to 250°F.

2. Toss the potatoes, onion, garlic, and rosemary sprigs with the olive oil. If making the short ribs, toss the potato mixture with the roasting ribs for the last hour of roasting and turn to coat with the meat's juices. Alternatively, put the potatoes in a roasting pan and roast, turning occasionally, for 1 hour, or until tender. Season with salt and pepper.

3. To serve, cut the potatoes in half.

## Roasted Artichoke Hearts

6 whole medium
artichokes

2 tablespoons extra-virgin
olive oil

1. Preheat the oven to 250°F.

2. To prepare the artichokes, remove the outer layers and cut out the heart.

3. Bring a large pot of water to a boil. Cook the artichoke hearts for 15 minutes, then drain.

4. Transfer to a medium bowl and toss with the olive oil. If making the short ribs, add the artichokes to the roasting pan with the ribs for the last hour of cooking. Alternatively, roast the artichokes separately in a roasting pan for 30 minutes.

# BRAISED SHORT RIBS WITH GINGER
# PORT RISOTTO
# GRILLED FRESH FIGS

Great for a crowd, this recipe is easy to double. Braising ensures the meat will be moist and tender and it creates a lovely sauce to spoon over the risotto. The ribs are typically sold three to a rack and can be separated before cooking, but I prefer to leave them whole. This helps retain the juices and makes for a spectacular presentation when they're paired with the magenta port risotto and grilled figs. **SERVES 6**

---

## Braised Short Ribs with Ginger

1 tablespoon olive oil

5 to 6 pounds short ribs

Freshly ground black pepper

1 large yellow onion, chopped

6 thin slices fresh ginger

4 garlic cloves, chopped

¼ cup soy sauce, plus more to taste

2 tablespoons fresh orange juice

1 tablespoon grated orange rind

**1.** In a Dutch oven or deep heavy pot, heat the oil over medium-high heat. Brown the short ribs for 10 to 15 minutes, turning constantly, until they are seared. Season with pepper.

**2.** Remove the ribs and pour off most of the fat. Lower the heat to medium and add the onion; cook, stirring, for 5 to 8 minutes, until soft.

**3.** Add the ginger and garlic and stir for 2 minutes. Add the soy sauce, orange juice and rind, and 1 cup water. Bring to a boil.

**4.** Return the ribs to the pot and reduce the heat to low. Cover and simmer, turning the ribs occasionally, for 1½ hours, until the ribs are very tender and the meat is falling off the bone.

**5.** Remove the ribs with a slotted spoon, set aside, and tent with aluminum foil. Discard the ginger slices. Raise the heat and boil the liquid for 5 to 10 minutes, until it is thick and syrupy. Taste and season with more soy if desired. Serve the sauce over the ribs.

# Port Risotto

2 tablespoons unsalted butter, divided

1 medium yellow onion, diced

1½ cups Arborio rice

1½ cups port

4 to 5 cups chicken stock, simmering

Salt and freshly ground black pepper

½ cup grated Parmesan cheese

¼ cup chopped fresh flat-leaf parsley, for garnish

**1.** In a large deep saucepan set over medium heat, melt 1 tablespoon of the butter and sauté the onion for 5 minutes, or until translucent, not letting it brown.

**2.** Using a wooden spoon, stir in the rice and coat with the butter. Cook, stirring, until the rice becomes translucent.

**3.** Slowly stir in the port and cook for 5 minutes, stirring until it's fully absorbed. Add 1 cup stock and simmer until absorbed, stirring frequently. Add the remaining stock, 1 cup at a time, allowing it to be absorbed before adding more and stirring frequently. Continue adding stock until the risotto is creamy.

**4.** Season with salt and pepper. Stir in the remaining butter and the cheese. Garnish with the parsley before serving.

TIP Always use a wooden spoon when making risotto. A metal spoon has hard edges that will break or crush the rice. The firmness of a risotto will vary depending on the freshness of the rice and the altitude at which it is cooked. In Southern California, where we're at sea level, the risotto cooks very quickly, and I have to be vigilant to make sure it's not overdone. In Colorado, it took longer!

# Grilled Fresh Figs

**12 fresh figs, cut in half**     **½ teaspoon olive oil**     **2 tablespoons balsamic vinegar**

**1.** Brush the figs with the oil.

**2.** Prepare a charcoal grill or preheat a gas grill to high and lightly sear the figs, cut side down, for 30 seconds. Flip and sear the other side for 30 seconds. Alternatively, heat a skillet over high heat and pan-sear each side of the figs for 30 seconds.

**3.** Transfer the figs to a bowl and toss them in the vinegar.

# POT ROAST
# HORSERADISH MASHED PARSNIPS AND POTATOES
# BURNT HONEY CARROTS

This meal is sheer comfort. The roast turns tender and silky as it simmers in an aromatic braise that yields a thick, smooth gravy, perfect for drizzling over the parsnip and potato mash. The burnt honey for these carrots is the result of a happy accident. I worried that I'd ruined a honey glaze by overcooking it, but once I tasted the carrots, I realized that slightly burning the honey gives it a deeper caramelized flavor. **SERVES 6**

## Pot Roast

1 3- to 4-pound chuck or rump roast, tied

Salt and freshly ground black pepper

2 tablespoons olive oil

1 cup chopped carrots

1 cup chopped onion

1 cup chopped celery

2 tablespoons tomato paste

1 cup red wine

1 cup beef stock

2 sprigs fresh rosemary

2 bay leaves

2 tablespoons unsalted butter

2 tablespoons chopped parsley

**1.** Preheat the oven to 300°F.

**2.** Pat the meat dry, and season with salt and pepper.

**3.** Film the bottom of a Dutch oven or roasting pan with the oil and set over high heat. Sear the roast, rolling it so that in 10 to 15 minutes all sides are well browned. Remove the roast and set aside.

**4.** Add the carrots, onion, and celery to the pan and sauté for 10 minutes, or until the vegetables are golden. Stir in the tomato paste and cook for 1 minute, or until it sticks and begins to brown.

**5.** Add the wine and stock to deglaze the pan, scraping up all the little dark nubs that cling to the bottom, then add just enough water to cover the vegetables.

(continues)

**6.** Put the roast back in the Dutch oven or roasting pan with the vegetables; add the rosemary and bay leaves. Cover the roast with aluminum foil. Cook for 1½ to 2½ hours, turning every hour. Cooking time will depend on the thickness and shape of the roast; it is ready when a fork will pierce the meat without pushing too hard and the juices run clear.

**7.** Remove the pan from the oven, set the roast on a carving board, and tent with aluminum foil. Tip the pan and strain the juices into a saucepan. Discard the vegetables, rosemary sprigs, and bay leaves.

**8.** Set the pan over medium heat and bring to a simmer. Reduce the liquid by half. Swirl in the butter and season with salt and pepper. Slice the roast and serve drizzled with the sauce and garnished with the parsley.

## Horseradish Mashed Parsnips and Potatoes

| | | |
|---|---|---|
| 2 pounds parsnips, peeled and cut into 2-inch pieces | 3 tablespoons unsalted butter | 1 tablespoon prepared horseradish, or to taste |
| 3 medium russet or baking potatoes, peeled and cut into 2-inch pieces | ⅓ cup sour cream | Salt and freshly ground black pepper |

**1.** Put the parsnips and potatoes in a medium pot and add just enough water to cover. Bring to a boil over high heat, then reduce the heat to medium and simmer the vegetables for 7 to 10 minutes, until soft.

**2.** Tip out any excess water, put the vegetables in a food processor with the butter, sour cream, and horseradish, and puree. (If the parsnips seem stringy, run them through a food mill or strainer.) Season the puree with salt and pepper.

# Burnt Honey Carrots

**2 pounds carrots, peeled and cut into 2-inch pieces**

**3 tablespoons honey**

**2 to 4 tablespoons unsalted butter**

**Salt and freshly ground black pepper**

**1.** Put the carrots into a medium pot with just enough water to cover. Bring to a boil over high heat, then reduce the heat and simmer for 3 to 5 minutes, until the carrots are tender-crisp. Drain.

**2.** In a medium saucepan set over medium heat, cook the honey, watching carefully, until it begins to smell like caramel and starts to turn brown. Then pull from the heat immediately and stir in the carrots to coat.

**3.** Swirl in the butter to make a lush sauce. Season with salt and pepper.

# SHORT RIB SLIDERS WITH SPICY MUSTARD CREAM AND ONION-BACON JAM

This hearty sandwich makes good use of any leftover meat, but the short rib is especially flavorful. The Onion-Bacon Jam is smoky-sweet and horseradish hot. I like to serve this on a sweet Hawaiian bun, but any soft, fluffy bun will do nicely. It's the kind of easy comfort food to serve family and friends the day after a big party when you'd like help enjoying the leftovers. **SERVES 6**

½ cup sour cream

2 tablespoons extra-strong prepared horseradish

1 tablespoon Dijon mustard

6 ounces bacon, chopped

1 yellow onion, thinly sliced

1 cup packed brown sugar

½ cup apple cider vinegar

2 tablespoons maple syrup

2 pounds cooked short rib meat, shredded or chopped

Salt and freshly ground black pepper

12 Hawaiian sandwich buns

**1.** In a small bowl, whisk together the sour cream, horseradish, and mustard and set aside.

**2.** In a cast-iron skillet or frying pan set over medium heat, cook the bacon until the fat is rendered. Add the onion and cook for 4 to 6 minutes, until the onion is very soft. Stir in the brown sugar and cook for 2 minutes, or until melted. Stir in the vinegar and maple syrup and cook for 2 minutes, or until thick and syrupy.

**3.** Add the meat and cook for 2 to 3 minutes, or until it is thoroughly warmed through. Season with salt and pepper.

**4.** Split the buns in half and distribute the meat and jam over the buns. Top with the sour cream mixture and serve hot.

# PORK

There's nothing like a juicy pork chop or a sticky sparerib you can nibble off the bone. Mild-tasting yet succulent and juicy, pork is my go-to choice for entertaining because it's so easy to season and cook. When I was a kid growing up on our ranch, our neighbors raised hogs and often treated us to full pig roasts. We fought over the cracklings rendered as the meat sizzled and spit while it cooked over the open fire. Every little café in Santa Fe had a smoker fashioned out of an old oil drum to make its signature barbecue, and the aromas made you hungry just walking through town.

My grandmother always used that big cast-iron skillet to cook bacon and sear fatback. She'd save the rendered fat in a coffee can she tucked under the sink. She would make headcheese and sausages of the scraps left from the hogs our neighbors butchered. Little did she know that snout-to-tail cooking would be so trendy today. If you love bacon, wait until you try my Pork Belly (uncured bacon) Braised in Hefeweizen and Orange Peel. One thing I learned from those neighbors is that the breed of an animal makes a difference in the flavor and texture of its meat. Thank goodness today's farmers are raising heritage hogs such as Berkshire, Duroc, and Yorkshire, which are naturally plump.

## SELECTING PORK

In the United States, pork is not graded, so recognizing good-quality pork requires knowing what to look for in the various cuts. For big roasts, pork chops, and ribs, marbling is the surest clue to quality and flavor. The fat

# PAN-SEARED PORK TENDERLOINS
# GRANNY SMITH APPLE MASHED POTATOES
# ROASTED FENNEL RAGU

Pork, applesauce, and mashed potatoes were my favorite meal as a kid. Here, potatoes mashed with bits of Granny Smith apple pop with surprising tang. This homey trio is ideal for entertaining. Using a cast-iron skillet to sear the meat will ensure it has a good firm crust that seals in the meat's juices and keeps it tender. Use the same skillet to finish the fennel because the bits of seared meat will enrich the final sauce. The roasted fennel ragu adds a licorice note that pairs nicely with the sweet-tart apple. This upbeat dinner comes together quickly on a busy weeknight, but also makes a welcoming show for last-minute guests who want to hang out with you in the kitchen. **SERVES 6**

---

## Pan-Seared Pork Tenderloins

| | | |
|---|---|---|
| **2 pork tenderloins, 1 to 1½ pounds each** | **Salt and freshly ground black pepper** | **1 tablespoon unsalted butter** |
| | | **1 tablespoon olive oil** |

**1.** Preheat the oven to 350°F.

**2.** Pat the meat dry. Season it with salt and pepper. Set a cast-iron skillet or large heavy sauté pan over high heat. Add the butter and oil and cook for 1 minute, or until the butter turns light brown (watch that it doesn't burn).

**3.** Put 1 or both tenderloins in the pan (do not crowd the pan) and sear for 4 to 6 minutes, rolling from side to side until the meat is nicely browned.

**4.** Transfer to a rack set over a baking sheet and roast in the oven for 10 minutes, or until an instant-read thermometer reaches 145°F. Remove and allow the pork to rest for 10 minutes before slicing into medallions.

## Granny Smith Apple Mashed Potatoes

6 medium russet or baking potatoes, peeled and cut into 2-inch pieces

2 tablespoons unsalted butter

½ cup heavy cream

2 Granny Smith apples, cored and cut into small dice

Salt and freshly ground black pepper

**1.** Put the potatoes in a medium pot with enough water to just cover. Bring to a boil over high heat, reduce the heat to medium, and simmer the potatoes for 7 to 10 minutes, until very soft.

**2.** Tip out the excess water and put the potatoes in a food processor with the butter and cream. Puree the potatoes.

**3.** Add the apples and pulse until they are finely chopped into the potatoes. Season with salt and pepper.

## Roasted Fennel Ragu

4 fennel bulbs, fronds removed and saved for garnish

2 tablespoons olive oil, divided

12 cherry tomatoes

1 teaspoon chopped fresh flat-leaf parsley

1 cup chicken stock

1 tablespoon unsalted butter

Salt and freshly ground black pepper

**1.** Preheat the oven to 350°F.

**2.** Cut the fennel bulbs in half horizontally and toss with 1 tablespoon of the olive oil. Place flat side down on a baking sheet. Roast for 30 minutes, or until very tender.

**3.** Remove from the oven, transfer to a cutting board, and slice.

**4.** Film a cast-iron skillet or heavy sauté pan with the remaining 1 tablespoon oil and set over medium-high heat. (If making the tenderloin, use the pan the pork was seared in.) Sauté the fennel with the tomatoes and parsley for 3 minutes.

**5.** Add the stock and cook, stirring occasionally, for 10 to 15 minutes, until the liquid is reduced by half. Swirl in the butter. Season to taste. Garnish with the fennel fronds.

# GRILLED PORK T-BONE
# CREAMY HORSERADISH POTATO GRATIN
# GRILLED BALSAMIC RED ONIONS

Mix a few cocktails and gather your friends around the grill at sunset. This dinner is casual and quick. The center-cut or pork loin chop includes a large T-shaped bone, similar to the beef T-bone. Bone-in chops tend to be juicier because the bones help the meat retain its moisture. Horseradish loses most of its fire but not its flavor when heated, and it gives this creamy gratin a gentle kick. Grill these tangy-sweet onions just as you're finishing the pork chops to serve on top for a final flourish.

**SERVES 6**

## Grilled Pork T-Bone

**Rahm's Brine for Pork (page 84), made 1 day ahead**

**6 T-bone pork chops**

**2 tablespoons olive oil**

**1.** One day before cooking, brine the pork (see page 84).

**2.** Prepare a gas or charcoal grill or preheat the broiler to high.

**3.** Remove the pork chops from the brine, rinse, and pat dry. Coat the chops with oil. Grill the chops for 6 minutes, flip, and continue grilling for another 6 minutes, or until the internal temperature reaches 145°F on an instant-read thermometer.

**4.** Set on a rack over a platter and allow to rest for 15 minutes before serving.

# Creamy Horseradish Potato Gratin

**6 russet potatoes**

**2 tablespoons prepared horseradish**

**1 cup heavy cream**

**1 cup sour cream**

**½ cup grated Parmesan cheese**

**Salt and freshly ground black pepper**

**1.** Preheat the oven to 350°F.

**2.** Slice the potatoes ¼ inch thick, leaving the skin on.

**3.** In a medium bowl, whisk together the horseradish, heavy cream, and sour cream and add the potato slices.

**4.** In a 1-quart casserole or baking dish, arrange a layer of the potatoes, sprinkle with some of the cheese, and top with another layer of potatoes. Continue layering the potatoes and cheese. Finish by pouring any cream remaining in the bowl over the potatoes and sprinkling with the remaining cheese. Season lightly with salt and pepper.

**5.** Bake, uncovered, for 1 hour, or until the top is bubbly and the potatoes are cooked through.

**6.** Let rest for 3 to 5 minutes and cut into squares.


# Grilled Balsamic Red Onions

**1 cup balsamic vinegar**

**4 red onions, sliced ¼ inch thick**

**2 tablespoons unsalted butter**

**1.** Prepare a gas or charcoal grill or preheat the broiler to high.

**2.** In a medium saucepan, warm the vinegar over low heat.

**3.** Grill the onions for 1 minute per side or until tender and browned.

**4.** Add the grilled onions to the vinegar and simmer for 10 minutes, or until the vinegar is reduced by half.

**5.** Whisk in the butter and serve over the pork.

# BACON-WRAPPED PORK MEDALLIONS
# SMOKED GOUDA POLENTA
# VEGETABLE PAVÉ

You can use a cast-iron skillet for this recipe to ensure that the bacon cooks up crisp, adding flavor to the milder pork tenderloins. Like beef filet mignon, pork tenderloin is the most delicate of all cuts. In fact, it is far leaner than beef. The bacon also gives the meat a smoky, salty edge that works beautifully with the soft, creamy smoked Gouda polenta. A pavé resembles lasagna but uses thinly sliced vegetables in place of pasta. This combination of eggplant, summer squash, and zucchini is an inspired version of ratatouille. **SERVES 6**

## Bacon-Wrapped Pork Medallions

**2 large pork tenderloins, about 1 pound each**

**Salt and freshly ground pepper**

**12 strips bacon**

**1.** Pat the meat dry. Season with salt and pepper and slice each tenderloin crosswise into 6 medallions.

**2.** Wrap each medallion in a strip of bacon and secure with a toothpick.

**3.** Set a cast-iron skillet or large heavy sauté pan over medium-high heat and sauté the medallions in batches, for 5 minutes per side.

**4.** Transfer to a rack set over a platter and allow to rest for 10 minutes, or until the internal temperature reaches 145°F on an instant-read thermometer.

# Smoked Gouda Polenta

1 tablespoon unsalted butter

1 white onion, chopped

1 quart chicken stock

2 sprigs fresh thyme

1 cup polenta

Salt and freshly ground black pepper

4 ounces smoked Gouda, shredded

**1.** In a large deep saucepan set over medium heat, melt the butter and sauté the onion for 5 minutes, or until translucent.

**2.** Stir in the stock and thyme and simmer over medium-low heat for 5 minutes. Remove the thyme.

**3.** Gradually whisk in the polenta in a slow, steady stream, working vigorously to prevent the formation of lumps.

**4.** When all of the polenta has been whisked in, reduce the heat to very low. Cook, whisking, for 5 minutes. Then stir occasionally with a wooden spoon for 20 to 25 minutes, until all of the liquid is absorbed. Season with salt and pepper.

**5.** Fold in the Gouda.

# Vegetable Pavé

| | | |
|---|---|---|
| **2 zucchini** | **1 small red onion** | **½ cup ketchup** |
| **1 summer squash** | **2 to 3 tablespoons olive oil** | **¼ cup tomato paste** |
| **1 small or Japanese eggplant** | **1 garlic clove, chopped** | **1 cup balsamic vinegar** |

**1.** Preheat the oven to 350°F.

**2.** Cut the zucchini, squash, and eggplant into strips, and cut the onion into thin rings.

**3.** In a large skillet set over medium-high heat, add just enough oil to lightly film the pan. Sauté the zucchini strips for 3 to 5 minutes on each side, until wilted; remove and put in a large bowl. Repeat with the squash, then the eggplant, then the onion, working in batches so as not to crowd the pan and adding more oil if necessary.

**4.** Put the cooked vegetables in the large bowl.

**5.** In a medium bowl, whisk together the garlic, ketchup, tomato paste, and vinegar. Pour this mixture over the vegetables and toss to thoroughly coat.

**6.** Layer the coated vegetable strips in a 9 x 9-inch baking dish. Cover with plastic wrap and then with aluminum foil. Weight down with a second baking pan. Bake for 1 hour.

**7.** Remove the pan from the oven and carefully peel off the aluminum foil and plastic wrap. Cut the pavé into 6 squares.

# PISTACHIO-CRUSTED PORK CHOP MILANESE
# ROAST FINGERLING POTATOES
# WARM ARUGULA SALAD

Who doesn't love the classic Italian "Milanese"? It's the ideal meal to make ahead and finish off just as friends are sitting down at the table; they'll be wowed with this presentation. This recipe is cheaper, easier, and tastier than the traditional version made with veal. The pistachios add a little extra crunch and sweetness to the bread-crumb crust. Pounding the pork first helps to make it tender and cook quickly, and the bone in these chops provides a handle for nibbling off every last crunchy bit. Because the cast-iron skillet distributes the heat so evenly, it will ensure the crust gets crisp without any burning. Roasted fingerling potatoes help sop up some of the sauce while the fresh arugula adds a peppery note to the plate. **SERVES 6**

## Pistachio-Crusted Pork Chop Milanese

3 cups canned whole tomatoes, drained

2 garlic cloves

3 sprigs fresh thyme

1 small white onion, diced

1 teaspoon red pepper flakes

Salt and freshly ground black pepper

6 bone-in pork loin chops, 1½ inches thick

4 eggs

¼ cup whole milk

1 cup all-purpose flour

½ cup crushed pistachios

1 cup unseasoned dried bread crumbs

6 ounces grated Parmesan cheese

¼ cup olive oil, or more as needed

2 lemons, cut into large wedges

**1.** In a medium saucepan, crush the tomatoes with the back of a fork and add the garlic, thyme, onion, and red pepper flakes. Set over high heat and bring to a boil, then reduce the heat and simmer, uncovered, for 1 hour, or until the sauce is thickened.

**2.** Remove the thyme, pour the sauce into a blender or food processor fitted with a steel blade, and puree. Season with salt and pepper and set aside.

**3.** Preheat the oven to 350°F.

**(continues)**

**4.** Put the pork chops between plastic wrap on the counter. Using a wooden mallet, pound the pork chops, working from the outside to the middle, until they flatten to ½ inch.

**5.** In a medium shallow bowl, whisk together the eggs and milk. Season the flour with salt and pepper and spread it out on a plate. In a separate shallow bowl, toss together the pistachios, bread crumbs, and 4 ounces of the cheese. Dip the pork chops into the milk-egg wash, next the flour, then the milk-egg wash again, and then the bread crumb mixture. Set on a sheet of waxed paper or parchment.

**6.** Line two rimmed baking sheets with aluminum foil.

**7.** Generously coat the bottom of a cast-iron skillet or large heavy sauté pan with 2 tablespoons of the olive oil, and set over medium-high heat. When the oil shimmers, add 1 or 2 pork chops, but do not crowd the pan. Sear the pork chops for about 5 minutes on each side, until crusty brown. Place the cooked pork chops on the prepared baking sheets. Bake for 15 minutes, or until the internal temperature reaches 140°F on an instant-read thermometer.

**8.** Carefully ladle enough tomato sauce to cover all but a 1-inch border around the pork chops. Sprinkle the chops with the remaining cheese and return to the oven for 5 minutes, or until the sauce is warm and the cheese is bubbly. Serve with the lemon wedges on the side.

# Roast Fingerling Potatoes

18 to 24 fingerling
potatoes (3 to 4 pounds)

2 tablespoons extra-virgin
olive oil

1 teaspoon chopped fresh
rosemary

½ teaspoon coarse salt

Freshly ground black
pepper

**1.** Preheat the oven to 350°F.

**2.** In a large bowl, toss the potatoes with the olive oil, rosemary, and salt. Spread out on a rimmed baking sheet so the potatoes don't touch each other.

**3.** Roast, shaking the pan occasionally, for 30 to 40 minutes, until the potatoes are browned and tender. Season with pepper before serving.

# Warm Arugula Salad

2 tablespoons extra-virgin
olive oil

1½ pounds baby arugula

Juice of 1 lemon

Salt and freshly
ground black pepper

¼ cup shaved
Parmesan

**1.** In a cast-iron skillet, warm the oil over low heat.

**2.** Toss in the arugula and cook for 30 seconds, or until wilted. Season to taste with lemon juice, salt, and pepper and sprinkle the cheese over all. Serve immediately.

# RAHM'S BRINE FOR PORK

I use this brine for larger cuts of pork. It works well for poultry, too. It helps to tenderize the meat and keep it juicy while it cooks. Be sure the liquid is cold before immersing the meat. Once the meat has brined, rinse it well and pat dry. Discard the brine. **MAKES 2 QUARTS**

---

1 cup sugar

1 cup kosher salt

1 teaspoon whole cloves

1 teaspoon fennel seeds

1 tablespoon black peppercorns

1 tablespoon mustard seeds

5 bay leaves

2 cinnamon sticks

**1.** Put the sugar, salt, cloves, fennel, peppercorns, mustard seeds, bay leaves, cinnamon sticks, and 2 quarts water in a large pot. Set over high heat to warm, and stir for 3 minutes to dissolve the sugar and salt.

**2.** Cool to room temperature, then refrigerate so the brine is cold before adding the pork to brine for at least 8 hours or up to 1 day.

# PORK LOIN ROAST
## CASSOULET-STUFFED RED PEPPERS
# BRAISED GREEN CABBAGE

 This is my favorite roast, juicy and flavorful. I just can't keep from nibbling a little before it comes to the table. Searing off the meat in a cast-iron skillet first ensures the crust will be firm and flavorful, sealing in the meat's juices as it roasts. The roast is so simple and easy, you'll have plenty of time to make the stuffed peppers and luscious braised cabbage to go alongside. **SERVES 6**

## Pork Loin Roast

**Rahm's Brine for Pork (page 84), made 1 day ahead**

**1 3-pound boneless pork loin roast**

**3 garlic cloves**

**2 tablespoons olive oil**

**1.** One day before cooking, brine the roast (see page 84).

**2.** Preheat the oven to 350°F.

**3.** Remove the pork from the brine, rinse, and pat dry.

**4.** Using a thin-bladed knife, cut slits into the roast. Insert the garlic cloves into the slits.

**5.** Heat the oil in a cast-iron skillet over medium-high heat and sauté the roast for 7 to 10 minutes, rolling it back and forth so it browns on all sides.

**6.** Place the pork on a rack in a roasting pan and roast for 30 minutes, or until an instant-read thermometer reaches 140°F. Remove from the oven and allow to rest for 20 minutes before carving into thick slices.

# Cassoulet-Stuffed Red Peppers

½ pound dried white beans

1 white onion

3 garlic cloves

6 large red bell peppers

5 strips bacon, chopped

1 teaspoon dried sage

3 ounces blue cheese

1 tablespoon olive oil

**1.** One day before cooking, rinse the beans, place in a large pot, and add water to cover by 2 inches. Let soak for at least 6 and up to 8 hours.

**2.** Drain the beans, rinse, return to the pot, and again cover with water by 2 inches. Add the onion and garlic and set the pot over high heat. Bring to a boil, reduce the heat, and simmer the beans, partially covered, for 60 to 90 minutes, until very tender. Remove and discard the onion and garlic, drain, and set aside.

**3.** Cut the peppers in half horizontally. Remove the seeds and veins. Set aside.

**4.** Preheat the oven to 350°F.

**5.** In a cast-iron skillet set over medium-high heat, cook the bacon for 5 minutes, or until the fat is rendered and the bacon begins to crisp. Turn off the heat and add half of the beans, breaking the beans to create a smooth paste, then gently fold in the remaining beans with the sage and blue cheese.

**6.** Stuff the pepper halves with the bean mixture, arrange in a baking dish, drizzle with the olive oil, and bake for 15 to 20 minutes, until the tops of the peppers are bubbly.

# Braised Green Cabbage

**3 tablespoons unsalted butter**

**1 large or two small heads green cabbage, trimmed, cored, and cut into 3-inch wedges**

**1 cup chicken stock**

**1 sprig fresh thyme**

**1 bay leaf**

**Salt and freshly ground black pepper**

**1.** In a cast-iron skillet set over medium-high heat, melt the butter. Add the cabbage and sear the cut sides for 3 minutes each, until both sides are deep brown.

**2.** Add the stock, thyme, and bay leaf. Reduce the heat to a simmer, cover the skillet, and cook for 5 minutes, or until the cabbage is tender. Season with salt and pepper.

TIP  Be sure to sear the cabbage well so that the cut sides are well darkened. This caramelizes the vegetable's sugars and gives it a deep, flavorful crust.

# APPLE AND PANCETTA PORK ROULADE
## CAMBOZOLA BARLEY RISOTTO
# BRAISED ENDIVE

Pork roulade is the first dish I tackled early in my career, signaling my step up from a cook to a chef. Not all pork loins look alike; some are thicker than others and require more pounding. However, don't worry about how ragged the pork looks after it's butterflied and pounded. Once cooked, its slices swirled with the stuffing will look elegant. The barley, cooked risotto-style, gets a rich finish from the Cambozola, a triple-cream French version of Gorgonzola cheese. The endive, braised in butter, is silky and mild. **SERVES 6**

## Apple and Pancetta Pork Roulade

1 3- to 4-pound pork loin

1 Granny Smith apple, cored and chopped

2 ounces pancetta, chopped

1½ cups toasted, cubed baguette

1 cup chopped yellow onion

1 tablespoon chopped fresh sage

1 egg

Salt and freshly ground black pepper

1 tablespoon olive oil

**1.** Pat the meat dry. Set the loin on a cutting board and with a sharp knife, make a cut down the length of the pork loin (but NOT cutting all the way through), working to within 1 inch of the cutting board. Open the pork flat so it resembles a large rectangle. If the slabs seem too thick, cut each of them in half again, starting from the center and working outward so the meat resembles a fold-out book.

**2.** Using the flat side of a mallet or a rolling pin, pound the sides to ½ inch thick. Lay out plastic wrap that is wide enough to extend past the sides of the pork by 4 inches. On top of the plastic wrap lay out 4 or 5 lengths of kitchen string that extend 6 inches on either side of the pork. Lay the pork, cut side up, on top of the strings on the plastic wrap.

(continues)

**3.** In a medium bowl, toss together the apple, pancetta, bread, onion, and sage. Add the egg and mix in thoroughly. Spread the filling evenly over the top of the pork. Starting from the wide side, roll the meat into a compact cylinder, tucking the stuffing inside as you go. (You can also simply fold the pork in half along the "hinge.")

**4.** To tie the rolled meat, begin with the middle string, make a triple knot, and work outward from the middle tie. Make the second and third ties 2 inches from either side of the first. Tie just tightly enough to hold the roll together, but do not cinch too tightly. Wrap the pork in the plastic and put it in the freezer for 1 hour.

**5.** Preheat the oven to 350°F.

**6.** Sprinkle the pork with salt and pepper.

**7.** In a large heavy skillet set over medium-high heat, add the oil and heat until shimmering. Sear the pork, carefully rolling it from side to side, for 10 minutes, or until it has a good firm crust.

**8.** Place the pork on a rack in a roasting pan and roast for 45 minutes to 1 hour, or until an instant-read thermometer inserted into the center of the roast registers 140°F. Remove from the oven, tent loosely with aluminum foil, and let rest for 15 minutes. Snip the strings and cut crosswise into thick slices to serve.


## Cambozola Barley Risotto

1 tablespoon unsalted butter

1 white onion, chopped

1 cup pearl barley

1 cup white wine

4 to 5 cups chicken stock, simmering

4 ounces Cambozola cheese

1 tablespoon sliced fresh basil

Salt and freshly ground black pepper

**1.** In a large saucepan set over low heat, melt the butter, then add the onion and sauté for 5 minutes, or until translucent.

(continues)

**2.** Add the barley, white wine, and 2 cups of the stock and bring to a boil. Reduce the heat and simmer, stirring, for 5 minutes, or until most of the stock is absorbed. Add the remaining stock, ½ cup at a time, allowing the stock to be absorbed before adding more, stirring frequently and covering the pot between additions of stock. The total cooking time will be 30 to 40 minutes, until the barley is tender.

**3.** Fold in the Cambozola and basil, and season to taste with salt and pepper.

## Braised Endive

| | | |
|---|---|---|
| 3 tablespoons unsalted butter | Salt and freshly ground black pepper | 1 sprig fresh thyme |
| 6 Belgian endives, trimmed, damaged leaves removed, halved lengthwise | 2 cups low-sodium chicken stock | |
| | 1 bay leaf | |

**1.** Melt the butter in a large heavy skillet over medium heat. Place the endives cut side down in the skillet and cook for 5 minutes, or until golden brown. Turn the endives over and cook for 3 to 5 minutes, or until brown on the other side. Sprinkle with salt and pepper, and add the stock, bay leaf, and thyme.

**2.** Cover the pan, reduce the heat, and cook on low for 15 to 20 minutes, or until the endives are very tender and easily pierced with a knife. Remove the cover and continue simmering until the liquid is reduced to a sauce.

**3.** Remove the bay leaf and thyme sprig. Serve the endives with the sauce spooned on top.

# CUMIN-CRUSTED PORK LOIN
## ISRAELI COUSCOUS WITH FETA AND JALAPEÑO
# TEQUILA-LIME CORN AND JICAMA SLAW

The Latin tango of flavors—cumin, cilantro, lime—spark these three simple recipes to make a bright plate that's as colorful as it is delicious. This pork loin is my go-to for entertaining friends. Be sure get the cast-iron skillet plenty hot to ensure a good firm sear on the pork so that it roasts quickly to be tender and juicy. The zesty salad may be made a day ahead. **SERVES 6**

## Cumin-Crusted Pork Loin

Rahm's Brine for Pork (page 84), made 1 day ahead

1 2-pound boneless center-cut pork tenderloin with thin layer of fat, tied

1 tablespoon freshly ground black pepper

1 tablespoon crushed cumin seeds

2 tablespoons olive oil

**1.** One day before cooking, brine the pork (see page 84).

**2.** Preheat the oven to 350°F. Remove the pork from the brine, rinse, and pat dry.

**3.** In a small bowl, toss together the pepper and cumin, then turn out onto a plate. Roll the pork in the seasoning so it's thoroughly coated.

**4.** Film a cast-iron or other large heavy skillet with the oil and set over medium-high heat. Sear the pork for 7 to 10 minutes, rolling it from side to side to create a dark, thick crust.

**5.** Set the pork on a rack in a roasting pan and cook in the oven for 30 minutes, or until the internal temperature reaches 145°F on an instant-read thermometer. Remove the pan from the oven and allow the pork to rest at room temperature for 15 minutes before carving into thick slices.

## Israeli Couscous with Feta and Jalapeño

1 tablespoon salt, plus more to taste

2 cups Israeli couscous

2 tablespoons olive oil

1 small red jalapeño pepper, seeded and diced fine

1 small red onion, diced

¼ cup crumbled feta cheese

2 tablespoons chopped fresh flat-leaf parsley

¼ cup chopped fresh cilantro

Freshly ground black pepper

**1.** In a large saucepan, bring 2 quarts of water to a boil and add the tablespoon of salt. Add the couscous and cook, stirring occasionally, for 8 to 10 minutes, or until tender. Drain and rinse under cold running water.

**2.** In a large sauté pan, heat the oil over high heat and sauté the pepper and onion for 2 to 3 minutes, or until tender. Stir in the couscous, toss to coat, and cook for 1 minute to heat through. Stir in the feta, parsley, and cilantro. Season with salt and pepper to taste.

## Tequila-Lime Corn and Jicama Slaw

1 cup cooked corn kernels

½ pound fresh jicama, coarsely grated

1 red onion, shredded

½ small green cabbage, shredded

1 tablespoon olive oil

Juice of 2 limes

2 ounces tequila

3 tablespoons chopped fresh cilantro

Salt and freshly ground black pepper

**1.** In a large bowl, toss together the corn, jicama, onion, and cabbage.

**2.** In a small bowl, whisk together the olive oil, lime juice, and tequila.

**3.** Toss the dressing with the vegetables, mix in the cilantro, then season with salt and pepper. Allow the salad to stand at room temperature for at least 15 minutes before serving so the flavors marry.

# PORK ADOVADA
# SPANISH RICE
# ZUCCHINI, EGGPLANT, AND CORN LASAGNA

This recipe is inspired by my grandmother's spicy-sweet pork stew. As soon as she'd get the pork searing in her big cast-iron skillet, we knew we were in for a fabulous dinner, though we'd have to be patient and wait a few hours. My grandmother always served this favorite meal with plenty of Spanish rice, a delicious sticky blend of rice, tomatoes, and onions. Use the same skillet the pork was seared in to cook the bacon for the rice. It distributes the heat evenly, ensuring that the bacon will be crispy and the tomato paste will caramelize without burning. This is the perfect dish for a Sunday dinner after a lazy afternoon. In this lasagna recipe, thinly sliced vegetables take the place of pasta and are layered with creamed corn and cheese.

**SERVES 6**

## Pork Adovada

**4 pounds pork butt or shoulder roast, cut into 2-inch pieces**

**½ cup New Mexican or red chile powder**

**1 teaspoon ground cumin**

**Salt and freshly ground black pepper**

**1 tablespoon olive oil**

**1 white onion, diced**

**1 tablespoon chopped garlic**

**1 cup chicken stock**

**1 tablespoon dried oregano**

**1.** In a large bowl, toss the pork with the chile powder, cumin, and salt and pepper and allow to stand at room temperature for 1 hour.

**2.** Heat the oil in a cast-iron skillet or large sauté pan until it shimmers. Add the pork and sauté for 5 minutes, turning often so that all sides are nicely seared. Transfer the pork to a slow cooker.

**3.** Return the skillet to the stove, add the onion and garlic, and cook for 3 to 5 minutes, or until softened. Add the stock and oregano, scraping up the dark nubs, and bring to a boil.

(continues)

**4.** Pour the stock and onion over the pork and add water if necessary to barely cover the meat. Cover and cook the pork on low for 5 to 6 hours, or until very tender.

> TIP
>
> This can be cooked in the oven in much less time. Preheat the oven to 250°F. Put the seared pork in a baking dish or an ovenproof casserole; pour the cooked onions and stock over the pork. Cover and bake for 3 hours, or until the pork is very tender. Cooked this way, the meat is a little less moist and tender, though the flavors are still wonderful.

## Spanish Rice

4 strips bacon, chopped

1 white onion, diced

1 cup long-grain white rice

2 tablespoons tomato paste

2 cups chicken stock

1 jalapeño pepper, seeded and diced

1 cup canned diced tomatoes with juice

2 tablespoons chopped fresh cilantro

**1.** Set a cast-iron skillet or a sauté pan over medium-high heat and sauté the bacon and onion for 5 to 10 minutes, until the bacon has rendered its fat and the onion is wilted. Remove the bacon and set aside.

**2.** Add the rice and toss to coat it with the bacon fat, then stir in the tomato paste, cooking for 15 to 30 seconds to brown.

**3.** Whisk in the stock, scraping up any brown bits that have clung to the bottom of the pan. Stir in the pepper and the tomatoes with their juices. Cover the pot, reduce the heat so the liquid simmers, and cook the rice for about 30 minutes, stirring occasionally, until tender.

**4.** Remove the lid, toss in the cilantro, and garnish with the cooked bacon.

# Zucchini, Eggplant, and Corn Lasagna

1 tablespoon unsalted butter, softened

2 cups corn kernels, fresh or frozen

1 cup heavy cream

Salt and freshly ground black pepper

1 zucchini

1 summer squash

1 medium eggplant (1½ pounds)

1 red onion

1 cup shredded Monterey Jack cheese

**1.** Preheat the oven to 350°F. Lightly butter a 9 x 13-inch baking dish or casserole.

**2.** In a small saucepan set over medium heat, stir together the corn and cream and simmer for 5 minutes, until the kernels are very tender.

**3.** Transfer to a blender or food processor fitted with a steel blade and puree. Season with salt and pepper and set aside.

**4.** Cut the zucchini, squash, and eggplant lengthwise into very thin strips and the onion into thin slices. Lay several of these strips across the bottom of the baking dish, then spoon on some corn-cream mixture and sprinkle with some of the cheese. Continue layering the vegetables with the corn mixture and cheese to fill the dish, finishing with the corn mixture and sprinkling with the cheese. Cover with a layer of plastic wrap and cover the plastic wrap with aluminum foil.

**5.** Bake for 45 minutes to 1 hour, or until the vegetables are cooked through and the top is bubbly. Remove the pan from the oven, peel off the foil and the plastic, and return to the oven for an additional 5 minutes to brown the cheese.

# HEFEWEIZEN BRAISED PORK BELLY
# BRIE MAC AND CHEESE
# CILANTRO-GLAZED CARROTS

Pork belly is uncured, unsmoked bacon. No wonder. It's unctuous, flavorful, and very easy to cook. Don't be put off by the amount of pork needed; the meat shrinks dramatically as it cooks. Be sure to use a cast-iron skillet to sear it first so the little bits of crusty pork left in the skillet can be made into the luscious sauce with Hefeweizen (a wheat beer). It packs a spicy, citrusy kick and cooks into a lovely glaze for this tender cut. The mac and cheese is surprisingly delicate and a cinch to whip up, perfect with the light, bright glazed carrots. **SERVES 6**

## Hefeweizen Braised Pork Belly

**4 pounds pork belly**

**½ cup chopped white onion**

**½ cup chopped carrot**

**½ cup chopped celery**

**2 12-ounce bottles Hefeweizen beer**

**1 cup chicken stock**

**1 bay leaf**

**1 sprig fresh thyme**

**Peel and juice of 1 orange**

**Salt and freshly ground black pepper**

**1.** Preheat the oven to 220°F.

**2.** Set a cast-iron skillet or large heavy sauté pan over high heat and sear the pork, fat side down, for 5 minutes, then flip and sear the second side for 5 minutes, creating a thick brown crust on both sides. Transfer the pork to a plate and set aside.

**3.** Add the onion, carrot, and celery to the pan and sauté over medium heat for 5 minutes, or until the onion is golden brown. Stir in the beer, scraping all the dark nubs off the bottom of the pan, then stir in the stock. Add the bay leaf, thyme, and orange peel and juice.

(continues)

# BORRACHO SPARERIBS WITH CHIPOTLE GLAZE
# GRILLED PAPAS BRAVAS
# LIME-CILANTRO CORN ON THE COB

You'll want meaty spareribs for this recipe. The glaze of tequila, honey, and chipotle peppers turns them crackling sweet and hot. They're partnered with crisped, paprika-spiked potatoes, called papas bravas, which the Spanish serve in tapas bars along with tangy lime-kissed corn on the cob. Roll up your sleeves; here's food you can eat with your hands. **SERVES 6**

---

## Borracho Spareribs with Chipotle Glaze

Rahm's Brine for Pork (page 84), made 1 day ahead

5 pounds country-style or St. Louis–style ribs

3 tablespoons honey

4 ounces tequila

2 tablespoons chopped chipotle peppers in adobo sauce

1 cup ketchup

¼ cup apple cider vinegar

**1.** One day before cooking, brine the ribs (see page 84).

**2.** Preheat the oven to 300°F.

**3.** Remove the pork from the brine, rinse, and pat dry.

**4.** In a large bowl, whisk together the honey, tequila, peppers, ketchup, and vinegar. Add the spareribs and turn them so they're completely coated with the sauce.

**5.** Lay two layers of aluminum foil on a baking sheet, cut double the length of the ribs. Lay a sheet of plastic wrap the size of the aluminum foil on top of that. Place the ribs on top of the plastic and foil (reserve the excess sauce), and fold up the sides to enclose the ribs in a packet. Put the ribs in a roasting pan and bake for 2 hours.

(continues)

**6.** Remove the baking sheet with the ribs. Carefully open the packet and pour the reserved sauce over the ribs. Return the uncovered ribs to the oven and continue baking for 30 minutes, or until they become brown and crisp. The meat will fall off the bone when they're done.

**7.** Prepare a charcoal grill, preheat a gas grill to high, or preheat the broiler to high.

**8.** Finish the ribs by setting them directly on the grill for 3 to 5 minutes, brushing with any remaining glaze, until they are nicely charred. Alternatively, place the ribs on a baking sheet or broiler pan, brush with the glaze, and broil for 3 minutes, or until nicely charred.

## Grilled Papas Bravas

| | | |
|---|---|---|
| **6 russet potatoes, peeled and cut into 3-inch wedges** | **2 tablespoons olive oil** | **Pinch of cayenne pepper** |
| **1 teaspoon salt** | **1 tablespoon smoked paprika** | **2 tablespoons finely grated Parmesan cheese** |

**1.** Put the potatoes in a large saucepan. Add the salt and just enough water to cover. Bring to a boil over medium-high heat, then reduce the heat and simmer the potatoes for 8 minutes, or until just tender. (Do not overcook.) Drain.

**2.** In a large bowl, whisk together the olive oil, paprika, and cayenne. Add the cooked potatoes and toss to coat.

**3.** Prepare a gas or charcoal grill to high.

**4.** Arrange the potatoes on the cooler part of the grill, near the perimeter, and grill for 8 to 10 minutes, turning until all sides are nicely seared.

**5.** Remove from the grill to another bowl and toss with the cheese. Serve hot.

# Lime-Cilantro Corn on the Cob

1 teaspoon sugar

6 ears fresh corn

2 tablespoons fresh lime juice

2 tablespoons chopped fresh cilantro

2 tablespoons mayonnaise

Salt and freshly ground black pepper

**1.** Set a large pot of water over high heat, add the sugar, and bring to a boil. Add the corn, reduce the heat, and cook for 10 minutes. Drain.

**2.** Prepare a gas or charcoal grill to high.

**3.** In a small bowl, whisk together the lime juice, cilantro, and mayonnaise. Rub the seasoned mayonnaise on the corn cobs.

**4.** Grill the corn, rolling constantly, for 5 minutes, or until nicely charred. Season with salt and pepper before serving.

> TIP The lime-kissed, cilantro-spiked mayo gives the corn a lovely tangy-sweet glaze as it grills. The mayonnaise is also delicious as a sandwich spread or served as a dip for vegetables.

# FIVE-SPICE BBQ PULLED PORK
## SESAME BROWN RICE CAKES
# CURRY PEAR SLAW

Once the pork is in the slow cooker, you're free for a good eleven hours while it simmers away into succulent, fork-tender shreds. The side of slaw adds more crunch and zing. This is a dinner we like to serve when we're all home; it's a family favorite. **SERVES 6**

## Five-Spice BBQ Pulled Pork

**2 cups chicken stock**

**1 cup pineapple juice**

**¼ cup packed dark brown sugar**

**¼ cup hoisin sauce**

**2 teaspoons five-spice powder**

**¼ cup balsamic vinegar**

**4 pounds pork shoulder roast**

**1.** Put the stock, pineapple juice, brown sugar, hoisin sauce, five-spice powder, and vinegar in a large slow cooker and stir to combine.

**2.** Add the pork and turn until the meat is coated with the liquid. Cover and cook on low heat for 10 hours.

**3.** Turn the lid so the pot is partially covered and continue cooking for 1 hour more.

**4.** To serve, transfer the meat to a platter and pull the meat into shreds with two forks.

# Sesame Brown Rice Cakes

1½ cups short-grain brown rice

1 teaspoon salt, plus more to taste

1 teaspoon dark sesame oil

¼ cup chopped fresh flat-leaf parsley

½ cup chopped scallions, both white and green parts

Freshly ground black pepper

1 cup sesame seeds, or more as needed

2 to 3 tablespoons olive oil, or more as needed

**1.** Put the rice and 1 teaspoon salt in a large pot with water to cover by about 1½ inches. Bring to a boil, then adjust the heat so the mixture bubbles gently. Cook, stirring occasionally and adding more water if the rice begins to stick to the bottom, until the grains are very tender and burst, about 1 hour.

**2.** Drain the rice and place in a large bowl. Stir in the sesame oil, parsley, scallions, and salt and pepper to taste and allow to cool thoroughly.

**3.** Preheat the oven to 350°F.

**4.** Pour the sesame seeds into a shallow bowl. Shape the rice mixture into 12 patties, about 3 inches wide and ½ inch thick. Pat each side of the patties in the sesame seeds to lightly coat.

**5.** Film a large skillet with the olive oil and set over medium-high heat. Fry the patties for 1 to 2 minutes per side, or until the sesame seeds are golden.

**6.** Transfer the patties to a baking sheet and bake for 5 minutes, or until hot.

# Curry Pear Slaw

1½ tablespoons yellow curry powder

¼ cup rice wine vinegar

1 tablespoon olive oil

½ teaspoon celery seed

½ cup whole-milk plain Greek yogurt

1 tablespoon honey

4 Bosc pears, unpeeled, cored and grated

1 head Napa (Chinese) cabbage, shredded

2 carrots, grated

1 red onion, julienned

½ cup chopped fresh cilantro

Salt and freshly ground black pepper

**1.** In a large bowl, whisk together the curry powder, vinegar, oil, celery seed, yogurt, and honey.

**2.** Toss in the pears, cabbage, carrots, onion, and cilantro. Season with salt and pepper. Serve cold.

> TIP  I use Greek-style (or strained) yogurt in place of mayonnaise when I want more tang and a lighter dressing.

# PORK BANH MI
# WITH PEANUT BUTTER AND CUCUMBER SALAD

Though there are many variations on banh mi, a Vietnamese sub sandwich, it always features fresh vegetable pickles and a fresh baguette. Leftover pork from any of my pork recipes will work nicely here. In my version, I substitute peanut butter for the classic paté to echo the creamy-rich texture with less fuss. To make the pickles, I slice the vegetables very thin using a vegetable peeler so they soak up the simple marinade. **SERVES 6**

---

1 pound cooked pork

1 cup rice wine vinegar

1 cup sugar

1 red onion, thinly sliced

1 cucumber, seeded and sliced lengthwise into thin strips

2 carrots, sliced lengthwise into thin strips

1 large fresh baguette

¼ cup good-quality peanut butter, crunchy or smooth

½ cup fresh cilantro leaves

**1.** Chop the pork and set aside.

**2.** In a medium bowl, whisk together the vinegar and sugar. Add the onion and marinate for 1 hour in the refrigerator.

**3.** Add the cucumber and carrots and marinate for 30 minutes, strain off the liquid, and save for later to drizzle over the top of the sandwich.

**4.** To assemble the sandwich, cut the baguette in half lengthwise. Open the baguette and spread both sides with the peanut butter. Layer on the pork, onion, cucumber, and carrots, then the cilantro. Drizzle with the reserved marinade.

**5.** Close the sandwich and slice into 6 equal sections.

PORK

# CHICKEN & TURKEY

Who can beat a picnic lunch of cold grilled chicken or a party on the deck with beer and spicy wings? Chicken is meat to please all. Whether it's white meat or dark, drumsticks or thighs, chicken is a sure bet. My favorite part of chicken and turkey is the crispy, flavorful skin. Thanks to our poultry farmers and producers, chicken and turkey are available in a variety of cuts.

You can take poultry meat in just about any direction because it's the most neutral, open to endless ethnic and cultural interpretation. Living in Southern California, I'm inspired by the gingery, sour, peppery Asian flavors, new to my Southwestern palate. When I hanker for an Indian curry, Korean hot pot, or Vietnamese stir-fry, poultry is the go-to meat. Of course, the classic roast chicken or turkey, cooked to a crackling brown and served with plenty of pan juices, will never let you down.

## SELECTING POULTRY

Start with good quality. Though chickens and turkeys are not graded, as beef is, you'll want to look for birds that are raised without antibiotics. When chickens are raised free-range, they are naturally healthy. Conventionally raised chickens are given massive doses of antibiotics to prevent the many diseases caused by living in such stifling confinement. Overuse of antibiotics in animals has become a major concern and has led to the widespread emergence of organisms that are resistant to antibiotic treatment. The more antibiotics we ingest through meat and from runoff into our groundwater, the more likely we will be to suffer from drug-resistant bacteria. Look for labels that read antibiotic-free or drug-free.

Kosher chickens and turkeys are salted before sale, which gives them a tighter, denser texture that is similar to that of brined meat (see page 84). One thing to note is that in Jewish tradition, the ritual slaughter depends on compassion for the animals and for many decades was the only humane method used to butcher poultry. The poultry is closely inspected to be sure the animal is not diseased, then is blessed.

The USDA label **"FREE RANGE"** applies only to poultry and ensures the birds have access to the outside. The definition of "outside" is relatively loose, however. It can be a wide backyard or a tiny patch of asphalt.

The **"USDA CERTIFIED ORGANIC"** label requires organic feed and prohibits antibiotics and cages. Because the farmer is forbidden to use drugs, the animals must be kept healthy, which generally means they roam in the fresh air. (Chickens contained in high-density environments will become ill.)

**"CERTIFIED HUMANE RAISED AND HANDLED"** is a program audited by the USDA. Chickens must be given more room to roam and have ventilation when inside.

**FRYERS/BROILERS AND ROASTERS** are terms often used to note size. Fryers or broilers are chickens under four pounds. Roasting chickens are larger, up to five or six pounds. The larger chickens can have tougher meat but generally have more flavor; they are best roasted or used for chicken soup or stew. Most markets carry smaller broilers or fryers that would work for any of these dishes.

# GENERAL RULES FOR COOKING POULTRY

- Poultry should always be cooked to at least 160°F because it can harbor salmonella, a bacterium that is killed at 160°F or higher. A meat thermometer is the best way to ensure an accurate temperature.

- Be sure to keep raw poultry away from other foods and to clean well the surfaces it has touched—cutting boards, countertops, and so on. (Be sure to wash cutting boards and knives right after working with raw poultry and before cutting other foods.)

- Use a cast-iron skillet when sautéing or frying chicken parts to ensure the meat sears to a firm crust and cooks evenly.

# CUTS OF POULTRY

Chicken and turkey are available in a wide range of different cuts, each suited to a different cooking method. Here they are at a glance.

**CHICKEN AND TURKEY BREAST MEAT,** the most popular cut, is sold whole, bone in or out, with the skin off or on, or divided into two halves, or sliced. Whole breasts may be stuffed and baked, roasted, or barbecued. Smaller breast fillets may be pan-fried or stir-fried. Whole breasts are best roasted skin on to retain moisture. Don't overcook; these dry out quickly.

**CHICKEN AND TURKEY THIGHS,** available bone in or out, are the tastiest parts. This is dark meat—it's firmer and more flavorful than white meat and requires more time to cook. Roasted or grilled whole, thighs are terrific slathered with a rich-tasting Southern barbecue or Asian sauce. The cutlets cook quickly when pan-fried or cut into strips for a stir-fry or tacos.

**CHICKEN DRUMSTICKS,** usually fried or barbecued, are meant for eating with your hands. Turkey drumsticks are terrific smoked.

**CHICKEN WINGS** have inspired entire restaurant chains. Roasted, barbecued, or grilled, these make easy party food (and they're the least expensive, too).

# ASIAN CHICKEN WINGS
# SESAME SOBA NOODLES
# CARROT-APRICOT SLAW

I've become fascinated by bold Asian flavors in my home in Southern California. I love to spend my off hours exploring the Asian neighborhoods in Los Angeles and their tiny mom-and-pop restaurants that serve Korean, Japanese, Thai, and Chinese food. I created this recipe to reflect the sticky sweet-tangy-spicy sauce that makes for remarkable chicken wings. These wings are hearty enough for an entrée but work nicely for an appetizer, too. The soba noodle salad can be made ahead. The slaw tastes even better the day after it's made. **SERVES 6**

## Asian Chicken Wings

**2 tablespoons chopped garlic**

**2 tablespoons hoisin sauce**

**1 tablespoon soy sauce**

**2 tablespoons fresh lime juice**

**2 tablespoons packed brown sugar**

**2 tablespoons olive oil**

**1 tablespoon dark sesame oil**

**Pinch of cayenne pepper**

**3 pounds chicken wings, tips trimmed off**

**2 tablespoons shredded unsweetened coconut**

**2 teaspoons chopped fresh cilantro**

**1 scallion, both white and green parts, finely chopped**

**1.** Preheat the oven to 425°F.

**2.** In a large bowl, whisk together the garlic, hoisin sauce, soy sauce, lime juice, brown sugar, olive oil, sesame oil, and cayenne. Add the wings and stir to coat.

**3.** Arrange the wings in one layer on a baking sheet, pour any remaining sauce over them, and roast, turning once, for 20 to 30 minutes, or until cooked through.

**4.** Sprinkle with the coconut and continue cooking for 5 more minutes, or until the coconut is lightly toasted.

**5.** Transfer the wings to a serving platter and garnish with the chopped cilantro and scallion.

CHICKEN & TURKEY

119

## Sesame Soba Noodles

¼ cup sesame seeds

10 ounces soba noodles

2 tablespoons dark sesame oil

2 tablespoons fresh lime juice

Salt and freshly ground black pepper

¼ cup sliced scallions, both white and green parts

**1.** Put the sesame seeds in a small skillet set over medium heat and toast, shaking the pan, for 1 to 3 minutes, until they are golden and smell nutty. Set aside.

**2.** Bring a large pot of water to a boil over high heat. Cook the noodles for 3 minutes, stirring with a fork to separate. Drain and transfer to a large bowl.

**3.** Toss the noodles with the oil, lime juice, and toasted sesame seeds. Season with salt and pepper to taste. Sprinkle with the scallions.

## Carrot-Apricot Slaw

¼ cup rice wine vinegar

2 tablespoons honey

½ teaspoon salt, plus more to taste

¼ teaspoon ground cumin

Pinch of cayenne pepper

½ cup chopped apricots

1 pound carrots, shredded

2 tablespoons olive oil

Freshly ground black pepper

2 tablespoons chopped fresh cilantro, for garnish

**1.** In a small pot set over medium heat, warm together the vinegar, honey, salt, cumin, cayenne, and apricots, then allow to cool.

**2.** In a medium bowl, toss together the carrots and olive oil. Season with salt and pepper and serve garnished with the cilantro.

# CHICKEN ARRABIATA WITH MUSHROOMS
# ROASTED NEW POTATOES
# BROILED BROCCOLINI

Directly translated, *arrabiata* means "angry" in Italian, but you're going to love this spicy tomato and mushroom sauce. Use a cast-iron skillet to first sear the meat so it leaves little bits of crust to enrich the sauce. It's perfect with the dark-meat chicken, and delicious spooned on the new potatoes. Use a colorful mix of new potatoes (often sold prebagged). Simply roasted in a little olive oil, they become nutty and tender. Broccolini, a more delicate broccoli with looser heads, is browned under the broiler until lightly caramelized and slightly sweet. **SERVES 6**

## Chicken Arrabiata with Mushrooms

6 whole chicken legs and thighs

Salt and freshly ground black pepper

1 tablespoon olive oil

¼ cup chopped white onion

2 garlic cloves, chopped

1 teaspoon red pepper flakes

¼ pound portobello mushrooms, cleaned (see Tip) and cut into ½-inch slices

¼ pound shiitake mushrooms, stemmed and cut in half

1 cup red wine

3 cups canned whole plum tomatoes, with juices

¼ cup slivered fresh basil

**1.** Season the chicken with salt and pepper.

**2.** Heat the oil in a cast-iron skillet or ovenproof sauté pan set over medium-high heat and sear the chicken on all sides for 8 to 10 minutes, until nicely browned. Remove the chicken and set aside.

**3.** Add the onion, garlic, red pepper flakes, and all of the mushrooms to the pan and sauté for 5 to 8 minutes, until they begin to smell nutty and turn brown. Stir in the wine and cook for 1 minute, scraping up any brown nubs. Stir in the tomatoes and basil.

**4.** Return the chicken to the pan and coat with the tomatoes. Cover the pan and simmer for 1 hour, until the chicken reaches 160°F on an instant-read thermometer.

> The best way to clean portobello mushrooms is to remove and discard the stems and, using a teaspoon or blunt knife, scrape away the gills under the cap. Rinse the mushrooms under cold running water, then drain on clean dish towels until thoroughly dry.

TIP

## Roasted New Potatoes

2 pounds mixed new potatoes (little red, Yukon gold, Yellow Finn), scrubbed but not peeled

5 garlic cloves, smashed

2 tablespoons olive oil

Coarse salt

**1.** Preheat the oven to 400°F.

**2.** Toss the potatoes with the garlic and enough olive oil to generously coat. Sprinkle with a little coarse salt. Spill the potatoes out onto a baking sheet so they're not touching.

**3.** Roast, shaking the pan occasionally, for 20 to 30 minutes, until very tender, golden brown, and slightly shriveled. Serve hot.

## Broiled Broccolini

1½ to 2 pounds broccolini, stems trimmed

2 tablespoons olive oil

Coarse salt

**1.** Preheat the broiler to high.

**2.** Bring a large pot of salted water to a boil. Blanch the broccolini for 1 minute, or until just tender-crisp. Drain and refresh under cold water. Pat dry.

**3.** Cut the broccolini into 2-inch strips. Toss with the oil and sprinkle with a little salt. Spread the broccolini out on a broiler pan and broil for 2 minutes per side, or until slightly charred.

# TURKEY KEBABS
## TZATZIKI COUSCOUS SALAD
## EGGPLANT CAVIAR

Yogurt makes a terrific marinade for lamb—the lactic acid helps make the meat tender and flavorful. In this kebab recipe, the natural sugars in the yogurt turn the meat a lovely caramel brown as it grills. I like to serve this with a couscous salad tossed with cucumber and mint, the classic ingredients in the Greek condiment tzatziki. Creamy eggplant caviar (baba ghanoush), a Mediterranean favorite, completes this plate that's great served with pita bread. Use six large or twelve small kebab sticks, and if they're wooden, be sure to soak them for two hours before grilling. **SERVES 6**

---

## Turkey Kebabs

3 pounds turkey breast

1 white onion, diced

3 garlic cloves, chopped

1 cup whole-milk plain Greek yogurt

¼ cup fresh lemon juice

1 teaspoon dried oregano

1 teaspoon ground cumin

Salt and freshly ground black pepper

2 red onions, cut into 2-inch pieces

2 red bell peppers, seeded and cut into 2-inch pieces

1 pound button mushrooms

**1.** A day before cooking, remove the bone and skin from the turkey and cut into 4-inch chunks. Put in a large nonmetallic bowl. Put the white onion, garlic, yogurt, lemon juice, oregano, and cumin in a food processor fitted with a steel blade or in a blender and puree. Season with salt and pepper. Pour the mixture onto the turkey and stir to coat. Cover and refrigerate overnight.

**2.** If using wooden kebab skewers, soak in water for 2 hours before grilling. Prepare a charcoal grill or preheat a gas grill to high. Put the red onions, peppers, and mushrooms in separate bowls. Thread the turkey chunks alternately with the vegetables onto 6 large or 12 smaller skewers. Grill, turning every 2 minutes, so all sides are seared (they cook quickly). Continue grilling and turning until the meat reaches 160°F on an instant-read thermometer. Set on a platter to serve with pita bread.

# Tzatziki Couscous Salad

1¾ cups couscous

2 cups chicken stock

Salt and freshly ground black pepper

½ cup whole-milk plain Greek yogurt

¼ cup fresh lime juice

1 tablespoon extra-virgin olive oil

½ cup peeled, diced cucumber

½ cup diced red onion

¼ cup diced radish

1 tablespoon chopped fresh parsley

1 tablespoon chopped fresh mint

**1.** Put the couscous in a large bowl.

**2.** Bring the stock to a boil, stir in a pinch of salt, then stir the stock into the couscous. Cover and let sit for 5 minutes, then fluff with a fork.

**3.** In a medium bowl, whisk together the yogurt, lime juice, and olive oil. Toss the cucumber, onion, radish, parsley, and mint with the couscous. Add the dressing and toss to lightly coat. Season with salt and pepper to taste.

# Eggplant Caviar

2 large eggplants

¼ cup plus 1 tablespoon olive oil

1 tablespoon chopped garlic

1 red onion, chopped

2 red bell peppers, seeded and chopped

½ cup balsamic vinegar

1 tablespoon tomato paste

Salt and freshly ground black pepper

**1.** Preheat the oven to 350°F.

**2.** Using a fork or a long, thin knife, poke holes all over the eggplants. Place them on a baking sheet and roast for 1 hour, or until shriveled and very tender. Remove and allow to cool.

**3.** In a deep sauté pan or cast-iron skillet, heat the 1 tablespoon oil over medium-high heat. Sauté the garlic, onion, and peppers for 10 minutes, or until very soft. Stir in the balsamic vinegar and cook for 2 to 3 minutes, or until it reduces to a thick syrup. Stir in the tomato paste.

**4.** Peel the eggplants and put them in a food processor fitted with a steel blade. Add the onion-pepper mixture with the syrup and pulse, then add the ¼ cup oil in a slow, steady stream, pulsing until the mixture is pureed. Season with salt and pepper. Transfer to a large bowl to serve.

# CHICKEN PUTTANESCA
# CREAMY PARMESAN HERB RISOTTO
# ROASTED GARLIC CAULIFLOWER

There are a lot of great stories that explain the name for this sauce, which translates to "whore's style" in Italian. It's a spicy dish, laced with garlic and heat; it gives whatever it kisses a powerful kick. Here it tops chicken breasts cut in what chefs call "airline style" (with their wings on). They land on a bed of creamy risotto and golden, roasted cauliflower. Be sure to use a cast-iron skillet so the chicken sears evenly for extra flavor before it's baked in the oven with the sauce. **SERVES 6**

## Chicken Puttanesca

3 whole chicken breasts, cut in half, with wings attached

Salt and freshly ground black pepper

1 tablespoon olive oil

¼ cup diced red onion

2 tablespoons chopped garlic

½ cup canned diced tomatoes with juice

¼ cup capers

¼ cup sliced kalamata olives

2 teaspoons red pepper flakes

½ cup chicken stock

½ cup white wine

1 tablespoon unsalted butter

**1.** Season the chicken with salt and pepper.

**2.** In a cast-iron skillet or large heavy sauté pan, heat the oil over medium heat. Sear the chicken, working in batches so as not to crowd the pan, for 5 minutes on one side. Flip the chicken and cook the other side for 5 minutes. Place the chicken in a large baking dish.

**3.** Preheat the oven to 350°F.

**4.** Put the onion and garlic in the pan the chicken was cooked in and sauté over medium-low heat for 3 to 5 minutes, or until the onion is golden. Add the tomatoes with their juices, capers, olives, red pepper flakes, stock, and wine and stir to combine. Simmer for 5 minutes, then swirl in the butter.

**5.** Spoon the sauce over the chicken and bake for 15 to 20 minutes, or until the internal temperature reaches 160°F on an instant-read thermometer. Serve immediately.

## Creamy Parmesan Herb Risotto

1 tablespoon unsalted butter

1 small white onion, chopped

1½ cups Arborio rice

½ cup white wine

5 to 6 cups chicken stock, simmering

2 tablespoons fresh thyme leaves

¼ cup chopped fresh flat-leaf parsley

¼ cup chopped fresh chives

Salt and freshly ground black pepper

¼ cup grated Parmesan cheese

**1.** In a large deep saucepan set over medium heat, melt the butter and sauté the onion and the rice for 3 to 5 minutes, or until the onion is soft.

**2.** Using a wooden spoon, stir in the white wine and cook for 1 minute, or until the liquid is absorbed by the rice. Slowly stir in 1 cup of the stock and cook until it is absorbed. Continue adding the stock, 1 cup at a time, stirring after each addition, until at least 5 cups of the stock have been absorbed by the rice over 15 to 20 minutes. Continue adding more stock if needed for a creamy rice.

**3.** Stir in the thyme, parsley, and chives. Season with salt and pepper. Fold in the Parmesan cheese. Serve hot.

## Roasted Garlic Cauliflower

¼ cup olive oil

2 small heads cauliflower, trimmed and quartered

2 tablespoons sliced garlic

Salt and freshly ground black pepper

**1.** Preheat the oven to 350°F.

**2.** In a cast-iron skillet, heat 2 tablespoons of the oil over medium heat and sauté the cauliflower for 2 to 3 minutes on each side, or until golden, then add the garlic and continue cooking for 1 minute, or until the garlic is soft.

**3.** Put the skillet in the oven and roast the cauliflower for 8 to 10 minutes, or until fork-tender. Season with salt and pepper.

# WAFFLE FRIED CHICKEN
# BUTTERMILK BISCUITS
# MAPLE-BACON COLLARDS

 This recipe marries two Southern favorites—fried chicken and waffles. The chicken's crust is crisp on the outside and tender within. A side of maple-bacon collards completes this classic meal. **SERVES 6**

## Waffle Fried Chicken

4 to 4⅓ pounds bone-in, skin-on chicken pieces

2 cups cake or pastry flour

1 teaspoon salt

2 teaspoons freshly ground black pepper

2 teaspoons paprika

1 teaspoon baking powder

1½ cups cold whole milk

3 to 4 quarts organic canola or vegetable oil

**1.** Rinse the chicken and pat dry. Separate the legs from the thighs and cut the breasts in half horizontally.

**2.** In a medium bowl, whisk together the flour, salt, pepper, paprika, and baking powder. Whisk in the milk to make a smooth batter. Let sit for 15 minutes so the baking powder activates.

**3.** Preheat the oven to 300°F.

**4.** In a large Dutch oven set over medium-high heat, heat the oil to 350°F so it shimmers. Dip the chicken pieces in the batter, allowing any excess to drip off into the bowl. Working in batches, fry the chicken in the oil (do not crowd the pot) for 10 to 15 minutes, turning occasionally, until it becomes a deep golden brown. Keep the oil at an even 350°F, checking it frequently with an instant-read thermometer, raising and reducing the heat as needed so the chicken cooks evenly and doesn't burn.

**5.** Place the chicken on a wire rack set over a baking sheet to drain, then bake for 10 to 15 minutes, or until the internal temperature of the chicken reaches 160°F on an instant-read thermometer.

# Buttermilk Biscuits

**2 cups cake or pastry flour**
**½ teaspoon salt**

**1 tablespoon baking powder**
**½ teaspoon baking soda**

**5 tablespoons cold unsalted butter, cut into bits**
**1 cup buttermilk**

**1.** Preheat the oven to 425°F.

**2.** Sift the flour, salt, baking powder, and baking soda into a large bowl. Using a pastry cutter, two knives, or your fingers, work in the butter to create a mixture that resembles small peas. Add the buttermilk and stir vigorously until the dough forms a ball.

**3.** Turn the dough out onto a lightly floured surface. Lightly knead until it's smooth. Pat the dough out into a rectangle roughly 8 × 7 inches and cut into 2-inch rounds. Place on an ungreased baking sheet and bake for 8 to 10 minutes, or until lightly browned. Serve immediately.

TIP Use cake or pastry flour for a tender biscuit and a light, crisp chicken crust. All-purpose flour will work, but not quite as well.

# Goat Cheese–Potato Croquettes

**1½ pounds russet potatoes, peeled and cut into chunks**

**Salt and freshly ground black pepper**

**½ cup whole milk**

**4 ounces goat cheese**

**2 tablespoons chopped fresh flat-leaf parsley**

**Pinch of freshly grated nutmeg**

**2 eggs, beaten**

**2 tablespoons to ¼ cup all-purpose flour**

**¼ cup vegetable oil, or more as needed**

**1 cup dried bread crumbs**

**1.** Put the potatoes in a deep medium saucepan. Add water to cover by 2 inches and a generous pinch of salt. Set over medium-high heat, bring to a boil, and cook for 15 minutes, or until the potatoes are very tender.

**2.** Drain the potatoes and transfer to a large bowl. With the back of a fork, mash in the milk, goat cheese, parsley, and nutmeg. Season with salt and pepper. Stir in the eggs and enough flour to allow the potatoes to hold their shape. Cover and refrigerate for 15 minutes.

**3.** Preheat the oven to 350°F.

**4.** Working with ¼ cup, scoop the potatoes out of the bowl and shape into cakes. Dredge the cakes in bread crumbs and set aside.

**5.** Pour ½ inch of oil into a cast-iron skillet or medium deep skillet and set over medium-high heat. Working in batches so as not to crowd the pan, fry the croquettes on each side for 5 minutes, or until browned.

**6.** Put the croquettes on a baking sheet and bake for 5 minutes. Serve warm.

## Fava Beans and Oyster Mushrooms

**1 pound shelled fresh fava beans**

**2 tablespoons unsalted butter**

**1 small white onion, chopped**

**1 pound oyster mushrooms, trimmed and rinsed**

**Salt and freshly ground black pepper**

**1.** Put the fava beans in a medium pot and cover with 2 inches of water. Set over medium-high heat, bring to a boil, and blanch the fava beans for 2 minutes.

**2.** Drain the beans in a colander and refresh under cold water. Remove the skin by pinching at the bottom of the bean to pop it out.

**3.** In a cast-iron skillet, melt the butter and sauté the onion for 5 minutes, or until translucent. Toss in the mushrooms and cook until tender and slightly brown, 5 to 8 minutes. Add the fava beans and cook for 1 more minute. Season with salt and pepper. Serve immediately.

> **TIP** Oyster mushrooms have a delicate flavor and creamy texture, but if they're not available, use cremini or shiitake mushrooms, stemmed and cut into 1-inch pieces, instead.

# TURKEY MOLE TOSTADAS
## BLACK BEAN CORN RAGU
## GRILLED LIME AVOCADOS

In my hometown, Santa Fe, every cook has his or her own special mole recipe, all with nuts, chiles, and chocolate. This recipe has evolved over time. It's easy enough for weeknight dinners but also makes a fine casual meal for a crowd. The black bean ragu is a lighter version of the spicy black bean stews I grew up eating. Grilling avocados caramelizes their sugars, making them taste especially sweet and nutty. You can make the turkey mole ahead; because the spices have had time to marry, it tastes even better the next day. These recipes are layered into the finished dish.

**SERVES 6**

## Turkey Mole Tostadas

3 tablespoons olive oil

3½ to 4 pounds turkey thighs

Salt and freshly ground black pepper

2 garlic cloves, smashed

1 white onion, diced

¾ cup unsalted raw peanuts, crushed

1 15-ounce can fire-roasted diced tomatoes with juice

½ 7-ounce can chipotle chiles in adobo sauce

½ cup pineapple juice

½ teaspoon cinnamon

1 ounce bittersweet chocolate, roughly chopped

1 quart chicken stock

18 tostadas, to layer

½ cup sour cream

¼ cup chopped fresh cilantro

**1.** Preheat the oven to 375°F.

**2.** Drizzle 1 tablespoon of the oil over the turkey and season with salt and pepper. Place the turkey on a roasting rack set over a roasting pan and roast for 35 to 45 minutes, until the meat is tender and the juices run clear. Remove from the oven, allow to cool, remove the skin and bones, and shred the meat.

**3.** While the turkey is roasting, film a Dutch oven or large deep skillet with the remaining 2 tablespoons of oil and set over medium-high heat. Sauté the garlic, onion, and peanuts for 3 minutes, or until the garlic is just golden and aromatic.

(continues)

**4.** Stir in the tomatoes, chiles, pineapple juice, cinnamon, chocolate, and stock, stirring until the chocolate melts and the mixture becomes smooth. Reduce the heat and simmer, covered, for 10 to 15 minutes. Transfer to a blender and puree.

**5.** Return the sauce to the pot and stir in the shredded turkey.

**6.** Place a tostada on each plate, add a layer of black bean ragu, a tostada, a layer of the turkey mole, and another tostada, then top it all with the grilled avocados and onions. Garnish with a dollop of sour cream.

## Black Bean Corn Ragu

| | | |
|---|---|---|
| 1 pound dried black beans or turtle beans | 1½ cups corn kernels, fresh or frozen | Salt and freshly ground black pepper |
| 1 quart chicken stock | 1 jalapeño, seeded and chopped | ¼ cup chopped fresh cilantro |
| 1 white onion, chopped | | |

**1.** The day before cooking the beans, put them in a large bowl and cover with cold water by 2 inches. Let stand overnight, then drain and set aside.

**2.** Put the beans, stock, and onion in a large deep pot. Set over high heat, bring to a boil, and reduce to a simmer. Cover and cook for 20 to 30 minutes, or until the beans are tender. Drain all but 1 inch of liquid from the pot. Smash the beans with the back of a fork, then stir in the corn and jalapeño.

**3.** Set over medium heat and cook for 3 to 5 minutes, stirring, until the corn is tender but still crunchy. Season with salt and pepper and stir in the cilantro before serving.

## Grilled Lime Avocados

3 large ripe avocados, peeled and cut in half lengthwise

1 red onion, sliced

¼ cup fresh lime juice

¼ cup tequila

2 tablespoons olive oil

½ teaspoon ground cumin

Salt and freshly ground black pepper

**1.** Prepare a gas or charcoal grill or preheat the broiler to high.

**2.** Place the avocados and onion slices on the grill and turn every 30 seconds so that all sides are nicely charred. Transfer to a large bowl.

**3.** In a small dish, whisk together the lime juice, tequila, olive oil, and cumin. Add the dressing to the avocados and onion and gently toss to coat. Season with salt and pepper.

# HUNTER'S CHICKEN
# OLIVE-CRUSTED POTATOES
# GREEN BEAN SALAD IN MUSTARD VINAIGRETTE

When I get home at night from a busy day, I want to be around friends and I want the cooking to be simple and the food homey and good. I rely on my cast-iron skillet and favorite recipes like this chicken. Also known as chicken cacciatore, it tastes even better the next day when the flavors have had a chance to marry. The olive-crusted potatoes sop up the fragrant sauce. The robust chicken and rich potatoes call for a tangy vegetable; snappy beans in peppery mustard vinaigrette do the trick.

**SERVES 6**

## Hunter's Chicken

1 tablespoon olive oil

2½ to 3 pounds bone-in skin-on chicken thighs or mixed chicken parts

1 white onion, chopped

4 garlic cloves, chopped

2 cups canned diced tomatoes with juice

½ cup red wine

2 sprigs fresh rosemary

Salt and freshly ground black pepper

¼ cup chopped fresh flat-leaf parsley, for garnish

**1.** In a cast-iron skillet or large sauté pan, heat the oil over high heat and add the chicken. Brown for 5 minutes on each side. Remove and set aside.

**2.** Reduce the heat, add the onion, and cook for 5 minutes, or until tender. Add the garlic, tomatoes, wine, and rosemary. Raise the heat to medium-high and cook, stirring occasionally, for 5 minutes.

**3.** Return the chicken to the skillet and turn in the liquid to coat. Cover, reduce the heat to medium-low, and simmer, turning occasionally, for 30 minutes, or until the chicken reaches 160°F on an instant-read thermometer. Season to taste with salt and pepper. Serve garnished with the parsley.

## Olive-Crusted Potatoes

12 medium red potatoes

Salt and freshly ground black pepper

1 cup kalamata olives, drained

½ cup fresh bread crumbs, toasted

2 tablespoons extra-virgin olive oil

**1.** Preheat the oven to 350°F.

**2.** Bring a large pot of water to a boil and cook the potatoes for 15 minutes, or until tender when poked with a knife. Drain. Using the back of a fork, smash the potatoes in the pot, season with salt and pepper, then transfer to a baking dish.

**3.** Pit the olives, chop them fine, and put them in a small bowl. Toss in the bread crumbs. Spread the olive and bread crumb mixture over the potatoes and drizzle with the oil. Bake for 10 minutes, or until the top is golden brown.

## Green Bean Salad in Mustard Vinaigrette

1 pound green beans, tips removed

2 tablespoons Dijon mustard

2 tablespoons white wine vinegar

1 tablespoon fresh lemon juice

¼ cup extra-virgin olive oil

Salt and freshly ground black pepper

**1.** In a large pot of rapidly boiling water, blanch the green beans for 2 minutes, or until bright green and tender-crisp. Drain, transfer to a large bowl, and cover to keep warm.

**2.** In a small bowl, whisk together the mustard, vinegar, and lemon juice, then slowly whisk in the oil. Toss the beans with enough vinaigrette to coat. Season with salt and pepper. Serve warm or at room temperature.

# CHICKEN (OR TURKEY) FOCACCIA SANDWICH WITH PESTO

 This is a star sandwich. It's perfect for the picnic basket (with a nice chilled wine) for a day on the beach and it's great with a beer watching a ball game at home. It makes easy use of leftover chicken or turkey, combining it with fragrant pesto and golden raisins. I add in crunchy pine nuts, too, and while they can be pricey, a little here goes a long way, and I think they're worth it. **SERVES 6**

2 garlic cloves

Juice of 1 lemon

½ cup olive oil

8 ounces fresh basil leaves

2 ounces grated Parmesan cheese

4 ounces pine nuts, toasted (see Note)

Salt and freshly ground black pepper

1 pound cooked chicken or turkey, shredded or diced

2 ounces golden raisins

1 loaf of focaccia

**1.** Put the garlic, lemon juice, and oil into a blender and process until smooth. Pulse in the basil, cheese, and 2 ounces of the pine nuts until just combined. Season with salt and pepper. Set aside.

**2.** In a medium bowl, toss together the chicken or turkey and raisins, then add enough of the basil mixture to generously coat. Stir in the remaining pine nuts.

**3.** Split the focaccia loaf in half horizontally and spread the chicken mixture evenly over the bottom half. Place the other half on top. Cut into 6 wedges to serve.

NOTE   To toast the pine nuts, spread them on a rimmed baking sheet and toast in a preheated 350°F oven for 3 minutes, or until golden.

# LAMB

In our family, lamb is the meat for special occasions—Easter, Christmas, birthdays; even on Thanksgiving we ate lamb. The scent of roasting lamb sparks the memories of very special meals. To this day, I make lamb to celebrate everything from a good report card to a special anniversary. My favorite Valentine's Day dinner is two pretty little lamb chops grilled to perfection.

The spring lamb my grandfather raised and served for our family's Easter dinner was roasted in the big fireplace he built in his backyard. I'd help him barbecue the ribs, braise the shanks, and grill the legs and loin. My grandmother cooked the whole head to serve with her fiery red and green chile sauces. The tables were laden with side dishes of Spanish rice, pinto beans, pozole, and grilled corn, enough to satisfy all thirty of us. We'd dig in after the Easter egg hunt that sent kids and adults scurrying all over the ranch. Desserts of bread pudding and très leche were followed by a game of gin rummy for the men.

Lamb is one of the most sustainable meats, requiring little land for pasture. When raised outside, it's naturally healthy. With more interest in local food and the growth in small, integrated farms that raise sheep, lamb is becoming a more popular option to cook at home. It is available in a variety of cuts similar to beef and pork. Ground lamb makes a great addition to meatloaf, burgers, and meatballs.

## SELECTING LAMB

New Zealand, Australia, and Colorado are the world's prime areas for raising sheep, and they produce excellent lamb. But they're all slightly different in flavor, texture, and cooking qualities.

# PAN-SEARED LAMB CHOPS
## POTATO GNOCCHI WITH MASCARPONE SAUCE
## STUFFED PORTOBELLO MUSHROOMS

Here's a simple dinner for a Valentine's Day party. You can divvy up the kitchen responsibilities, cook together, and serve this in a candlelit dining room. Purchase individual chops or get your hands on a cheaper rack and cut them yourself. To make the gnocchi, use high-starch baking potatoes, as they have the driest texture. The kosher salt draws the moisture up to the potato's surface, creating a fluffy interior. You can make these ahead and hold them overnight or freeze them to enjoy later. While gnocchi have a reputation for being fussy, with this easy recipe, you'll be turning them out like a pro. **SERVES 6**

## Pan-Seared Lamb Chops

| | | |
|---|---|---|
| **12 to 18 French lamb chops, depending on size** | **Salt and freshly ground black pepper** | **1 to 2 tablespoons olive oil** |

**1.** Preheat the oven to 350°F.

**2.** Pat the lamb dry. Season the chops with salt and pepper on both sides.

**3.** Film a cast-iron skillet or large frying pan with the oil and set over medium-high heat. Sear the chops for 3 minutes, or until the outside is golden and crusted, then flip and sear the other side for 3 minutes.

**4.** Place the chops on a baking sheet and roast for 8 to 10 minutes, or until the internal temperature reaches 125°F on an instant-read thermometer for rare chops or 135°F for medium.

# GRILLED LAMB T-BONES WITH SAUCE VERT
# PARSNIP CROQUETTES
# POACHED LEEKS

Just the dinner for a Labor Day grilling party, this menu is a festive salute to summer. It's hearty enough with the pretty parsnip croquettes to welcome in fall. Be sure to use the cast-iron skillet to fry them—it will ensure the croquettes cook through evenly and don't burn. T-bones are meaty chops perfect for grilling, but sometimes the little pocket near the bone remains raw. To prevent this, press on the bone when you first place the chop on the grill to heat it quickly. The bright green, fresh sauce vert comes together quickly and is delicious drizzled over the lamb, parsnip croquettes, and mild leeks to bring together all the flavors on this plate. **SERVES 6**

## Grilled Lamb T-Bones with Sauce Vert

12 to 18 lamb T-bones, depending on size

Salt and freshly ground black pepper

1 cup chopped shallots

1 bunch scallions, white parts only, chopped

¼ cup chopped fresh flat-leaf parsley

¼ cup olive oil

2 tablespoons sherry vinegar

**1.** Prepare a gas or charcoal grill or preheat the broiler to high.

**2.** Pat the lamb dry, and season with salt and pepper. For rare lamb, grill for 3 to 5 minutes per side, or until the internal temperature is 125°F; for medium, cook for another 2 minutes per side, or until the internal temperature reaches 135°F.

**3.** In a food processor fitted with a steel blade or a blender, puree the shallots, scallions, parsley, olive oil, and vinegar. Season with salt and pepper. Drizzle over the lamb before serving and pass additional sauce on the side.

# LAMB MEDALLIONS
# SWEET POTATO GALETTE
# CRUSTY FRIED GREEN TOMATOES

Lamb medallions are a great way to kick off the weekend on a Friday night with an easy casual dinner with friends. The sweet potato galette sounds far more extravagant than it actually is. Invite your friends into the kitchen to help assemble the galette and fry the tomatoes. The tomato recipe comes from my grandmother, one she created to use up those hard green tomatoes when the garden was winding down. Lamb medallions are cut from the tender loin and, like a fine filet mignon, need to be handled with care. This simple meal makes for an artful presentation with the colorful sweet potato galette and crispy green tomatoes. **SERVES 6**

## Lamb Medallions

**4 lamb loins, 3½ pounds each, each cut into 18 medallions**

**Salt and freshly ground black pepper**

**2 tablespoons olive oil**

**1.** Pat the lamb dry, and season with salt and pepper.

**2.** Film a cast-iron skillet or a large sauté pan with the oil and set over medium-high heat. Sear the lamb for 5 minutes to create a good, hard crust, then flip and sear for another 5 minutes, or until the internal temperature reaches 125°F for rare or 135°F for medium.

# Sweet Potato Galette

**¼ cup (½ stick) unsalted butter**

**1 teaspoon chopped fresh thyme**

**4 large sweet potatoes, peeled**

**½ cup chopped onion**

**Salt and freshly ground black pepper**

**1.** Preheat the oven to 350°F.

**2.** Melt the butter in a large cast-iron skillet (see Tip) over medium heat and add the thyme. Pour into a medium bowl.

**3.** Slice the potatoes ⅛ inch thick, discarding the ends. Put the potato slices in the bowl with the butter and toss well to thoroughly coat.

**4.** Arrange potato slices and half of the onion over the bottom of the cast-iron skillet in a concentric pattern, overlapping them slightly. Sprinkle with salt and pepper. Arrange another layer of potatoes and the remainder of the onion over the first layer, sprinkling with more salt and pepper. Repeat until you've used all the potato slices.

**5.** Cover the skillet with foil and bake for 45 minutes, or until a fork pierces easily through the layers. Serve the galette cut into wedges.

TIP  When making the Sweet Potato Galette, use the same skillet the lamb was cooked in. Layer the sweet potato slices in the unwashed skillet.

# Crusty Fried Green Tomatoes

3 eggs

1 cup buttermilk

6 large green tomatoes

1 cup all-purpose flour

Salt and freshly ground
black pepper

1 18-ounce box corn flake
cereal, crushed fine

1 cup vegetable oil

**1.** Preheat the oven to 350°F.

**2.** Whisk the eggs and buttermilk together in a small bowl and
set aside.

**3.** Remove the top and bottom inch of the tomatoes, then cut the
tomatoes into 1-inch slices.

**4.** Season the flour with salt and pepper and spread in a high-sided
plate. Put the crushed cereal in a separate high-sided plate.

**5.** In a large deep skillet set over high heat, bring the oil to 350°F so
it's shimmering. Dredge the tomato slices in the seasoned flour; dip
them in the egg mix, then dredge them in the corn flakes.

**6.** Working in batches, fry the tomato slices on one side for
3 minutes, turn, and continue frying for another 2 minutes.

**7.** Set on a baking sheet and keep warm in the oven until all the
slices are fried. Serve immediately.

# LAMB PARMESAN WITH MINT-TOMATO SAUCE
# ORZO WITH CHÈVRE
# STOVETOP RATATOUILLE

Here's an easy recipe that may be prepped ahead of time and finished just before guests arrive. The flavor of the lamb works beautifully with the Mediterranean flavors in this dish. Add the mint just as the sauce finishes simmering so it will taste bright and fresh. The orzo with chèvre is a surprisingly tangy and light twist on the more familiar mac and cheese—the perfect partner to the sunny ratatouille. **SERVES 6**

## Lamb Parmesan with Mint-Tomato Sauce

3 cups canned plum tomatoes, with juice

2 fresh basil leaves

1 white onion, chopped

2 tablespoons chopped fresh mint

Salt and freshly ground black pepper

2 lamb tenderloins, 1¾ pounds total

3 eggs

1 cup whole milk

1 cup all-purpose flour

2 cups dried bread crumbs

2 tablespoons olive oil

¼ cup grated Parmesan cheese

**1.** Put the tomatoes, basil leaves, and onion in a large pot and set over medium-high heat. Bring to a boil, reduce the heat, and simmer for 1 hour. Fold in the mint and season with salt and pepper.

**2.** Preheat the oven to 350°F.

**3.** Pat the lamb dry, and cut each of the tenderloins into 3 pieces, horizontally. Using a meat mallet or a heavy rolling pin, pound each piece ½ inch thick.

**4.** In a shallow bowl, whisk together the eggs and milk and set aside. Season the flour with salt and pepper and spread it out on a plate. Season the bread crumbs as well and spread them on a separate plate. Dredge the lamb in the seasoned flour, dip in the egg mix, then dredge in the bread crumbs.

**5.** Film a cast-iron skillet or large heavy sauté pan with the oil and set over medium-high heat. Sear the medallions for 3 minutes on each side. Transfer the medallions to a rimmed baking sheet.

(continues)

# PAN-SEARED LAMB LOIN
# HORSERADISH POTATO GRATIN
# SPAGHETTI SQUASH WITH BASIL AND ALMONDS

Lamb loin is a lean cut with a clean flavor that shines when simply pan-seared. My grandfather, who raised lamb on my mom's ranch in Santa Fe, saved the lamb loin for very special dinners with my grandmother, mother, and me. He would sear it in a cast-iron skillet, then we'd slather it with the chiles I helped my mom and grandma roast over an open fire. My grandfather liked strong flavors, and horseradish was one of his favorites, so we used it to season the lamb and potatoes. In this dinner, the rich and spicy horseradish potato gratin makes a hearty side dish that's nicely balanced by the light golden spaghetti squash with basil and toasted almonds.

**SERVES 6**

## Pan-Seared Lamb Loin

2 lamb loins, about 1½ pounds total

Salt and freshly ground black pepper

2 tablespoons olive oil

**1.** Pat the lamb dry, and season with salt and pepper.

**2.** Film a cast-iron skillet or large sauté pan with the oil and set over medium-high heat. Sear the lamb, rolling it back and forth, for 10 minutes, until crusty brown on all sides, or until the internal temperature reaches 125°F for rare or 135°F for medium on an instant-read thermometer. Allow the lamb to rest for 10 minutes before slicing into medallions.

## Horseradish Potato Gratin

1 tablespoon unsalted butter

1 cup heavy cream

2 tablespoons prepared horseradish

5 ounces goat cheese, crumbled

4 ounces Parmesan cheese, grated

Salt and freshly ground black pepper

5 Idaho or russet potatoes, peeled and sliced into ⅛-inch-thick rounds

(continues)

1. Preheat the oven to 350°F.

2. Generously grease a large baking dish with the butter.

3. In a medium bowl, whisk together the cream, horseradish, goat cheese, Parmesan cheese, and salt and pepper. Drop the potato slices into the cream mixture.

4. Arrange the potatoes in the baking dish and cover with plastic wrap, then place a layer of aluminum foil over the plastic wrap. Bake for 1 hour.

5. Remove the baking dish, uncover the potatoes, and discard the foil and plastic wrap. Return the dish to the oven and bake for 30 minutes, or until the top is crusty brown.

## Spaghetti Squash with Basil and Almonds

**1 large spaghetti squash**

**2 tablespoons olive oil**

**2 tablespoons sliced basil leaves**

**2 tablespoons chopped toasted almonds**

**Salt and freshly ground black pepper**

1. Preheat the oven to 350°F.

2. Poke several holes in the squash. Place the squash on a baking sheet and roast for 1 hour, or until the shell is soft.

3. Remove from the oven and cut the squash in half vertically. Set a large serving bowl in the oven just long enough to warm it. Using a fork, gently pull the strands from the shells, being careful to keep them intact.

4. Transfer to the warm bowl. Toss the squash with the oil, basil, and almonds and season with salt and pepper to taste.

# WHITE PEPPER–CRUSTED RACK OF LAMB
## CREAMY TRUFFLE PISTACHIO POTATOES
# GARLICKY OYSTER MUSHROOMS

I like to use Colorado lamb for this recipe. The racks are meaty, tender, and mild-tasting. When sealed in a peppery panko crust, the meat stays moist and juicy. Use a light hand when seasoning the potatoes with the truffle oil; a little goes a long way. Oyster mushrooms have a creamy texture and mild flavor that's enhanced with just a dab of butter. **SERVES 6**

## White Pepper–Crusted Rack of Lamb

2 racks of lamb

2 cups panko

1 tablespoon coarsely ground white pepper

3 tablespoons chopped fresh flat-leaf parsley

3 tablespoons Dijon mustard

¼ cup white wine

**1.** Preheat the oven to 350°F.

**2.** Pat the lamb dry.

**3.** In a medium bowl, mix together the panko, pepper, parsley, mustard, and wine. Spread the panko mixture over the lamb and set in a roasting pan.

**4.** Roast the lamb for 1 hour, or until the internal temperature reaches 125°F. Remove and set aside to rest before carving the rack.

## Creamy Truffle Pistachio Potatoes

6 russet potatoes, peeled and cut into 2-inch cubes

Salt and freshly ground black pepper

½ cup heavy cream

2 tablespoons unsalted butter

1 teaspoon truffle oil

¼ cup chopped toasted pistachio nuts

**1.** Put the potatoes in a large pot with enough water to cover by 2 inches and a generous pinch of salt. Set over high heat and bring to a boil. Cook the potatoes for 15 to 20 minutes, or until very soft. Drain and return to the pot.

**2.** Using a potato masher or sturdy whisk, whip in the heavy cream, butter, and truffle oil. Season with salt and pepper and fold in the nuts right before serving.

## Garlicky Oyster Mushrooms

1 tablespoon unsalted butter

1 tablespoon olive oil

1½ to 2 pounds oyster mushrooms, cut in half

1 tablespoon chopped garlic

1 tablespoon chopped fresh thyme

Salt and freshly ground black pepper

**1.** In a cast-iron or other large skillet set over medium-high heat, melt the butter with the oil.

**2.** Add the mushrooms, garlic, and thyme and cook, stirring, for 5 to 8 minutes, or until the mushrooms are very soft and lightly browned. Season with salt and pepper.

# LAMB OSSO BUCO
# COCONUT RISOTTO
# GRILLED JAPANESE EGGPLANT

This lamb recipe is easy to make ahead. In the summer, serve it with eggplant right off the grill. It's my version of the Italian classic, but with the warm notes of clove and cinnamon that work so well with this robust meat. Long, slow cooking yields a rich, glossy sauce that is terrific on the coconut risotto. The thin, quick-cooking Japanese eggplants, seasoned with fragrant dark sesame oil, are an easy yet flavorful side dish. **SERVES 6**

## Lamb Osso Buco

3 large lamb shanks

Salt and freshly ground black pepper

Pinch of ground cloves

2 tablespoons olive oil

1 cup chopped carrots

1 cup chopped white onion

1 cup chopped celery

3 garlic cloves

2 tablespoons tomato paste

1 cup red wine

2 cups chicken stock

1 cinnamon stick

2 tablespoons chopped fresh thyme

**1.** Preheat the oven to 275°F.

**2.** Ask the butcher to cut the shanks into 3-inch rounds. Pat the lamb dry, and season liberally with salt, pepper, and cloves.

**3.** Film a cast-iron skillet with the oil and set over medium-high heat. Working in batches, sear the lamb on all sides for a total of 10 minutes, so it's crusty and nicely browned. Transfer to a large Dutch oven or stew pot.

**4.** Add the carrots, onion, celery, and garlic to the skillet and sauté over medium heat for 10 minutes, until the vegetables are soft and nicely caramelized. Add the tomato paste and stir to coat the vegetables. Cook, stirring, for 5 minutes to brown slightly.

(continues)

**5.** Add the wine, scraping the drippings off the bottom of the pan with a wooden spoon. Reduce the wine by half, then add the stock, cinnamon stick, and thyme. Pour over the lamb and cover the pot.

**6.** Put the pot in the oven for 2 hours, turning the lamb every 30 minutes, until the meat is fork-tender and falling off the bone.

**7.** Remove the pot, take the lamb out of the sauce, and set aside on a serving platter. Remove the cinnamon stick. Pour the sauce into a blender and puree the vegetables. Serve the sauce over the lamb.

## Coconut Risotto

½ cup unsweetened coconut flakes

5 cups chicken stock

2 tablespoons unsalted butter

1 white onion, chopped

1½ cups Arborio rice

½ cup white wine

1 cup coconut milk

Salt and freshly ground black pepper

¼ cup chopped fresh cilantro, for garnish

**1.** Preheat the oven to 350°F.

**2.** Spread the coconut flakes on a small baking pan and toast for 2 to 3 minutes, or until just browned. Remove and set aside.

**3.** Pour the stock into a small saucepan and set over a low flame to bring to a gentle simmer.

**4.** In a large saucepan, melt the butter over medium-high heat and add the onion. Cook the onion, stirring with a wooden spoon, for 5 minutes, or until translucent. Stir in the rice and sauté for 1 minute. Add the wine and cook for 1 minute, or until evaporated.

**5.** Add 1 cup of the stock and simmer until it is absorbed by the rice, stirring frequently. Add the remaining stock 1 cup at a time, allowing the stock to be absorbed before adding more and stirring frequently. Slowly stir in the coconut milk. The total cooking time will be 30 to 35 minutes, or until the rice is creamy and tender.

**6.** Season with salt and pepper. Garnish with cilantro and coconut.

# Grilled Japanese Eggplant

**3 small Japanese eggplants, cut in half lengthwise**

**1 tablespoon olive oil**

**1 teaspoon dark sesame oil**

**1 to 2 tablespoons soy sauce, to taste**

**1.** Preheat a gas grill or prepare a charcoal grill.

**2.** Coat the eggplants with the olive oil and place cut side down on the grill. Grill for 6 to 8 minutes on one side, or until lightly charred and beginning to soften. Turn the eggplants, cover the grill, and continue cooking for another 6 to 8 minutes, until very tender.

**3.** Remove from the grill and drizzle the sesame oil and soy sauce over the cut sides of the eggplants. Serve hot.

> **TIP** These thin, Japanese eggplants are pretty, but you may also use a larger Italian eggplant cut into vertical strips.

# BRAISED LAMB SHANKS WITH MINT GREMOLATA
# MANGO AND PISTACHIO RICE
# ROASTED FENNEL

 The distinct robust flavor of New Zealand lamb is enhanced by the sweet apple juice and mellow rum in this long, slow braise. It's a good make-ahead meal, as the flavors marry while the meat rests after it's cooked. The dish is finished with a palate-cleansing lime gremolata, inspired by the Italian condiment that brightens traditional veal osso buco. I like to serve this on a bed of rice seasoned with dried mango. Roasted fennel adds a welcome anise note. **SERVES 6**

## Braised Lamb Shanks with Mint Gremolata

1 cup all-purpose flour

Salt and freshly ground black pepper

6 New Zealand lamb shanks

2 tablespoons olive or vegetable oil

1 cup chopped carrots

1 cup chopped onion

1 cup chopped celery

2 tablespoons tomato paste

2 cups chicken stock

2 cups unsweetened apple juice

1 cup sweet rum

¼ cup chopped fresh mint

1 tablespoon chopped garlic

Grated zest of 2 limes

1 tablespoon extra-virgin olive oil

**1.** Preheat the oven to 300°F.

**2.** Season the flour with salt and pepper and spread on a plate. Dredge the lamb shanks in the flour and shake off any excess.

**3.** Film a cast-iron skillet or large sauté pan with the olive or vegetable oil and set over medium-high heat. Working in batches, brown the lamb for 3 to 5 minutes, rolling to sear all sides until golden. Remove and set aside.

**4.** Add the carrots, onion, and celery to the pan and cook for 3 to 5 minutes, or until browned. Stir in the tomato paste and cook for 1 to 2 minutes, or until crusty brown and sticking to the bottom of the pan. Whisk in the stock, apple juice, and rum, scraping up any of the brown nubs that cling to the bottom of the pan.

(continues)

# LAMB GYROS
# WITH ROASTED RED PEPPERS, FETA,
# AND TZATZIKI SAUCE

 Be warned that in this classic Greek sandwich, loaded with roasted red peppers and salty feta, the tangy yogurt tzatziki sauce is sure to drip down your sleeve. Toast the pita or naan bread over a burner using tongs; if you try to warm them in the oven, they will become brittle and dry. **SERVES 6**

---

6 ounces whole-milk plain Greek yogurt

1 tablespoon fresh lime juice

1 tablespoon extra-virgin olive oil

1 tablespoon chopped fresh mint

1 tablespoon chopped fresh flat-leaf parsley

1 medium red onion, diced

1 small cucumber, peeled, seeded, and thinly sliced

Salt and freshly ground black pepper

6 pita or naan breads

2 bell peppers, roasted, or 1 cup jarred roasted red peppers, drained, sliced into ½-inch strips

1 pound cooked lamb, sliced thin

**1.** In a small bowl, whisk together the yogurt, lime juice, oil, mint, parsley, and most of the onion, reserving some for garnish. Stir in the cucumber and season to taste with salt and pepper. Set aside.

**2.** Using tongs, hold each pita over a flame or grill for 1 minute per side to char and warm. Open the bread on a plate.

**3.** Using tongs, roast the peppers over a gas flame for 3 minutes, turning them until they are just blistered on all sides. Alternatively, preheat a broiler to high and roast the peppers, turning occasionally, until all sides are blistered. Be careful not to overcook; just sear the skin. Place the peppers in a bowl and cover with plastic to cool. Carefully peel the peppers, being careful not to pierce them, then core and remove the seeds.

**4.** Fill the pitas or top the naan with the lamb, spoon in the sauce, top with the peppers, and garnish with the reserved onion. Serve right away.

# GAME

Come fall, the men in our family head out in their trucks to hunt antelope and game birds. As a kid, I went along, too, but I have to confess that I didn't love it. I had trouble sitting still and waiting and watching for long periods of time, hoping something would happen. For me, the best part of hunting was dealing with the game when we returned home. Butchering fascinated me. We used every part of the animal—from hide to hoof. My grand-dad and uncles taught me how to dress as well as cook the meat.

Most game tastes best when it's *not* overcooked. Game is lean yet its flavors are rich; it will taste "gamey" if not treated properly. Here's where a meat thermometer and a cast-iron skillet are essential. The heavy cast-iron skillet distributes the heat evenly so the meat cooks quickly with-out drying out and the thermometer provides accuracy.

These days, my game comes from my friends at Broken Arrow Ranch in central Texas. It's a collective of over a hundred ranchers who manage wildlife populations of veni-son, antelope, and wild boar that range in the wild, living on the abundant native grasses and herbs. In my travels across the country, I've met a number of small farmers and game farms that supply butchers and meat depart-ments with local game.

## SELECTING GAME

A growing number of game farms and ranches will ship game from online orders. You may also find select cuts of game at butchers and farmers' markets, and in some grocery stores. To be sure you are getting premium quality game, here's what to look for.

- Make sure the meat is USDA inspected. It will indicate this on the website and on any packaging. Any meat sold through a butcher, in a grocery store, or at a farmers' market must be processed by a USDA-inspected plant.

- Game birds such as duck, pheasant, quail, and goose should not have any odor. Their breasts should be plump and the meat firm.

- Game meat such as bison, venison, and boar should be pink or red and not have any odor. The rules are the same for buying most any meat. It should be finely grained with firm white fat.

## GENERAL RULES FOR COOKING GAME

Wild game and farm-raised game are similar, but there are a few key points of difference to remember.

- Wild game has the strongest flavor; farm-raised game is milder, but still more pronounced than domesticated animals. Adjust seasonings accordingly.

- Game is lean and easily overcooked.

- Brining game before cooking helps make it juicier and more tender; it also tempers the strong "gamey" flavor. (See Rahm's Brine for Pork, page 84.)

**FARM-RAISED GAME BIRDS** such as quail, pheasant, and duck are milder tasting than their wild cousins. Wild game birds are far leaner, so it's best to bard (wrap) them in bacon, pancetta, or prosciutto to add fat and flavor while they cook.

**VENISON AND ELK** are extremely lean. Both may be used in recipes calling for lean cuts of pork. Bigger cuts, from the shoulders or haunch, are best stewed or braised.

**BISON** (American buffalo) is very lean. These animals rely on their coats, not fat, to keep them warm in the winter. Because they are grass-fed, I find that the meat tastes just a bit sweeter than American beef. Be careful not to overcook bison, as it dries out quickly.

**WILD BOAR** is becoming popular because its flavor is richer and more distinct than that of farm-raised pork.

# PHEASANT WITH CHORIZO SAUSAGE
## FRESH CORN POLENTA
## SOUTHWEST CHAYOTE VEGETABLE SALAD

Don't let anyone try to tell you that pheasant tastes just like chicken, because it's better. I like to cook pheasant with the skin on to keep the meat juicy and moist. The spicy sausage in this dish creates a fragrant sauce that is delicious served on the polenta. The chayote tastes like a cross between cucumber and jicama and makes a great light salad. **SERVES 6**

## Pheasant with Chorizo Sausage

½ cup all-purpose flour

Salt and freshly ground black pepper

6 small boneless, skin-on pheasant breasts with wings attached

1 tablespoon unsalted butter

½ pound chorizo sausage, sliced ½ inch thick

½ cup chicken stock

**1.** Season the flour with salt and pepper. Dust the pheasant breasts with the seasoned flour and set aside.

**2.** In a cast-iron skillet or large sauté pan set over medium heat, melt the butter and cook the sausage for 5 to 8 minutes, turning so all sides brown. Remove the sausage, and set aside.

**3.** Add the pheasant to the skillet and sauté for 8 to 10 minutes, turning occasionally so all sides brown. Stir in the stock, scraping up all the brown nubs on the bottom of the pan, and simmer for 5 minutes, until the liquid is reduced and thickened.

**4.** Add the sausage back to the pan. Serve the pheasant on a bed of polenta topped with the sauce and sausage.

## Fresh Corn Polenta

3 cups fresh corn kernels

1 cup whole milk

2 tablespoons unsalted butter

1 white onion, chopped

3 cups chicken stock

1 cup coarse polenta

½ cup grated Parmesan cheese

Salt and freshly ground black pepper

**1.** In a food processor fitted with a steel blade or in a blender, puree 1 cup of the corn with the milk and set aside.

**2.** Set a deep saucepan over medium-high heat and melt the butter. Add the onion and sauté for 3 to 5 minutes, or until soft. Add the stock and bring to a simmer.

**3.** Slowly stir in the polenta and cook for 5 to 10 minutes, until it becomes a thick porridge. Stir in the milk and corn mixture and continue cooking the polenta, stirring, for another 5 to 10 minutes.

**4.** Fold in the remaining corn kernels, then fold in the cheese. Season with salt and pepper.

## Southwest Chayote Vegetable Salad

1 small cucumber, peeled, seeded, and cut into 1-inch dice

1 small chayote squash, cut into 1-inch dice

½ cup 1-inch diced jicama

½ cup quartered cherry tomatoes

1 avocado, cut into 1-inch dice

2 scallions, white parts only, chopped

¼ cup rice wine vinegar

¼ cup olive oil

1 tablespoon chopped fresh cilantro

½ teaspoon ground cumin

Salt and freshly ground black pepper

**1.** Combine the cucumber, chayote, jicama, tomatoes, avocado, and scallions in a large bowl.

**2.** In a small bowl, whisk together the vinegar and oil. Pour over the vegetables and gently toss to coat. Sprinkle in the cilantro and the cumin and season with salt and pepper.

GAME

# ROASTED QUAIL, GINGERSNAP STUFFING, AND PARSNIP POUTINE

 The quail I buy at my local market are boned and ready to be stuffed, making this elegant recipe far easier than it looks. Poutine, a traditional Canadian dish of French fries, beef gravy, and Cheddar cheese, inspired this medley—parsnip fries topped with lush, salty-sweet gravy and tangy chèvre. **SERVES 6**

## Roasted Quail with Gingersnap Stuffing

6 quail, boned

Salt and freshly ground black pepper

1 small baguette, diced

1 cup crumbled gingersnaps

2 tablespoons unsalted butter, softened

1 white onion, chopped

1 tablespoon chopped fresh sage

1 cup chicken stock

¼ cup sage leaves, for garnish

**1.** Preheat the oven to 350°F.

**2.** Rinse the quail inside and out and pat dry. Season with salt and pepper.

**3.** On a baking sheet, toast the baguette cubes in the oven for 5 to 10 minutes, until nicely dried. Turn into a big bowl and add the gingersnaps.

**4.** In a cast-iron skillet set over medium-high heat, melt 1 tablespoon of butter and sauté the onion for 5 to 8 minutes, until tender. Stir in the sage and stock. Add the onion mixture to the bowl with the bread and gingersnaps and season with salt and pepper.

**5.** Working from the front of the cavity, stuff the quail with the gingersnap mixture. Tie the front legs together with butcher's twine and tuck the wings under the back. Rub the quail with the remaining 1 tablespoon butter and set on a rack over a roasting pan. Roast for 20 to 25 minutes, or until the internal temperature reaches 160°F.

**6.** Remove the quail and rest it for 10 minutes; then remove the strings and serve whole. Garnish with the sage leaves.

# Parsnip Poutine

1 pound parsnips

2 tablespoons olive oil

1 cup chopped bacon

1 white onion, chopped

1 tablespoon packed brown sugar

1 tablespoon all-purpose flour

1 cup chicken stock

½ cup heavy cream

6 ounces chèvre, crumbled

1 bunch scallions, both white and green parts, thinly sliced

**1.** Preheat the oven to 400°F.

**2.** Scrub the parsnips and cut them lengthwise into strips, 1 inch wide by 2 to 3 inches long, so they resemble French fries. Toss the parsnips with the oil, turn out onto a baking sheet, and roast, turning occasionally, for 20 to 30 minutes, until tender and browned.

**3.** In a cast-iron skillet set over medium heat, cook the bacon to render the fat. Remove the bacon from the pan and set aside.

**4.** Return the pan to the stove, add the onion, and cook over medium heat, stirring, for 5 to 8 minutes, until the onion is soft. Stir in the sugar until it melts, then stir in the flour to make a thick paste and cook, stirring, for 1 minute. Whisk in the stock and bring to a simmer. Whisk in the heavy cream to make a thick sauce.

**5.** Remove the parsnips from the oven and serve topped with the gravy, cheese, and scallions. If you'd like, garnish the fries with the reserved bacon.

# CRISPY DUCK LEG CONFIT
# WARM POTATO SALAD
# CHILE-BRAISED NAPA CABBAGE
# WITH STRAWBERRIES

 Duck confit, duck legs cooked in fat, was created centuries ago as a means of preserving the meat. It's incredibly delicious. I like to pair confit with sharp flavors that cut through its richness. In these recipes, the sherry vinegar, strawberries, and habanero chiles do the trick. **SERVES 6**

## Crispy Duck Leg Confit

| 1 cup vegetable shortening | 2 sprigs fresh thyme | 6 duck legs |
| 4 bay leaves | 1 tablespoon black peppercorns | |

**1.** Preheat the oven to 250°F.

**2.** In a small pot, melt together the shortening, bay leaves, thyme, and peppercorns.

**3.** Put the duck legs in a baking dish and pour the shortening mix over them. Cover with plastic wrap and then with aluminum foil and bake for 3 to 4 hours, until a fork easily pierces the meat without any resistance. Remove and uncover the dish and allow the duck to cool in the fat for about 1 hour.

**4.** To serve, remove the duck from the pan and wipe the fat from the legs with a paper towel. Reserve ¼ cup of the fat to use in the potato salad.

**5.** Set a cast-iron skillet or large sauté pan over medium-low heat and add 1 to 2 tablespoons of the confit shortening, then cook the duck in batches so as not to crowd the pan. Brown the legs slowly, turning often, for 10 to 15 minutes, until crisp.

# Warm Potato Salad

6 Idaho potatoes

Salt and freshly ground black pepper

3 tablespoons sherry vinegar

1 tablespoon chopped fresh flat-leaf parsley

¼ cup fat from the Crispy Duck Leg Confit (preceding recipe) or extra-virgin olive oil

**1.** Use a 1-inch melon baller to scoop out potato balls, or peel and cut the potatoes into 3-inch chunks.

**2.** Bring a large pot of lightly salted water to a boil over high heat. Add the potatoes and cook for 5 minutes, or until just tender but not overdone. Drain and place in a large bowl.

**3.** In a small bowl, whisk together the vinegar, parsley, and duck fat and pour over the potatoes. Turn the potatoes to lightly coat. Season with salt and pepper and serve warm.

# Chile-Braised Napa Cabbage with Strawberries

2 tablespoons unsalted butter

2 small heads Napa (Chinese) cabbage, cored and thinly sliced

1 red onion, thinly sliced

¼ cup chicken stock

¼ cup white wine

1 teaspoon chopped seeded habanero chile

1 cup sliced strawberries

2 tablespoons chopped fresh cilantro

Salt and freshly ground black pepper

**1.** Set a cast-iron skillet or large deep sauté pan over medium-high heat. Melt the butter and add the cabbage and onion. Cook for 2 to 3 minutes, stirring constantly, until the vegetables are wilted.

**2.** Add the stock, wine, and habanero and continue cooking for 1 to 2 minutes, or until the cabbage is tender but still slightly crisp.

**3.** Stir in the strawberries and cilantro. Season with salt and pepper.

# ELK LOIN WITH PORT THYME BUTTER
# JALAPEÑO AND DRIED CHERRY SPOONBREAD
# HONEY-GLAZED TURNIPS

I love elk; it's bolder tasting than pork and leaner than beef. The tenderloin is like filet mignon, juicy and delicate. Here, the seared tenderloins are napped with ruby-colored, berry-scented port butter and served with spicy-sweet spoonbread that sops up all these fabulous juices. This recipe for honey-kissed turnips will convert the most stubborn root vegetable fiend. **SERVES 6**

## Elk Loin with Port Thyme Butter

1 cup port

1 sprig fresh thyme

½ cup (1 stick) unsalted butter, softened

3 pounds elk tenderloin

Salt and freshly ground black pepper

2 tablespoons olive oil

2 tablespoons parsley leaves, for garnish

**1.** In a small saucepan set over medium-high heat, bring the port to a simmer. Add the thyme and cook for 10 minutes to reduce the port by half.

**2.** Pour into a medium bowl and let cool to room temperature. Remove the thyme. Whip the butter into the port.

**3.** Pat the elk dry. Cut into 2- to 3-inch medallions and season with salt and pepper.

**4.** Film a cast-iron skillet or heavy sauté pan with the oil and set over high heat. Working in batches, sear the elk for 4 minutes on each side, or until an instant-read thermometer inserted into the center of a medallion registers 125°F to 130°F.

**5.** Serve each medallion with a dollop of the port butter. Pass the remaining butter on the side. Garnish with the parsley leaves.

## Jalapeño and Dried Cherry Spoonbread

2 tablespoons unsalted butter

1 white onion, chopped

2 jalapeños, seeded and diced

½ cup dried cherries

1 cup chicken stock

7 cups crumbled cooked cornbread

Salt and freshly ground black pepper

**1.** In a large deep skillet, melt the butter and sauté the onion and jalapeños for 5 to 8 minutes, until soft. Add the cherries and stock and bring to a simmer.

**2.** Gently fold in the cornbread. Season with salt and pepper. Serve warm.

> TIP    If I'm in a hurry, I use the baked cornbread our supermarket sells or I use a mix. Leftover corn muffins work nicely, too.

## Honey-Glazed Turnips

1 pound turnips

2 tablespoons unsalted butter

½ teaspoon cinnamon

2 tablespoons honey

Salt and freshly ground black pepper

1 tablespoon chopped flat-leaf parsley, for garnish

**1.** Preheat the oven to 350°F.

**2.** Scrub and trim the turnips. Cut them into 1-inch wedges. Set each wedge on a square of aluminum foil large enough to wrap it, then dot each turnip with a nob of butter, wrap into a packet, and place on a baking sheet. Bake the turnips for 1 hour, or until soft.

**3.** Open the packages, dump the turnips into a large bowl, and toss with the cinnamon and honey to coat. Season with salt and pepper and garnish with the chopped parsley.

# SEARED VENISON CHOPS WITH MARSALA
# WILD RICE PILAF
# ROASTED BUTTERNUT SQUASH

The only thing you need to know about cooking venison is not to overcook it. Here's where the cast-iron skillet is key. It allows you to cook the meat evenly over very high heat so the meat does not overcook, but stays juicy and tender. Venison resembles pork in flavor and texture, but it's richer and a little darker. It's complemented by a sauce of sweet wine, shallots, and piney sage; the wild rice, tasting of the deep north woods and clear lakes, is a perfect match. Seasonal butternut squash completes a fine autumn meal. **SERVES 6**

## Seared Venison Chops with Marsala

6 venison chops

Salt and freshly ground black pepper

2 tablespoons olive oil

3 tablespoons unsalted butter

6 large shallots, peeled

1 cup beef stock

1 cup Marsala wine

1 tablespoon chopped fresh sage

**1.** Pat the venison chops dry, and season with salt and pepper.

**2.** Set a cast-iron skillet over medium heat, add the oil, and sear the chops, without crowding the pan, for 4 to 5 minutes on one side. Flip and sear for 4 to 5 minutes on the second side, or until the internal temperature reaches 125°F on an instant-read thermometer. Remove and set aside.

**3.** In a large deep saucepan set over medium-high heat, melt 1 tablespoon of the butter and sauté the shallots for 5 to 8 minutes, turning so they brown on all sides. Stir in the stock, Marsala, and sage and simmer for 15 to 20 minutes, or until the liquid is reduced by half.

**4.** Swirl in the remaining 2 tablespoons butter, season with salt and pepper, and serve over the venison chops.

GAME

199

## Wild Rice Pilaf

| | | |
|---|---|---|
| 1 cup wild rice | Grated zest of 1 orange | ¼ cup chopped toasted walnuts (see Note) |
| 1 teaspoon unsalted butter | ¼ cup dried cranberries | |
| 2 shallots, minced | | Salt and freshly ground black pepper |

**1.** Rinse the wild rice under cold running water.

**2.** Put the rice and water to cover by 2 inches in a medium saucepan and bring to a boil. Reduce the heat, cover, and simmer for 45 minutes, or until the rice is tender. Drain any excess water from the rice.

**3.** Toss in the butter, shallots, orange zest, cranberries, and walnuts and season with salt and pepper to taste.

NOTE  To toast the nuts, preheat the oven to 350°F. Spread the walnuts on a baking sheet and toast in the oven for 3 to 5 minutes, or until they begin to darken and smell nutty. Remove, allow to cool, then chop.

## Roasted Butternut Squash

| | | |
|---|---|---|
| 1 large butternut squash | 2 tablespoons packed brown sugar | ½ teaspoon cinnamon |
| 1 tablespoon olive oil | | |

**1.** Preheat the oven to 350°F.

**2.** Peel and seed the squash and cut into 2-inch chunks.

**3.** In a large bowl, toss the squash with the oil and then the sugar and cinnamon. Spread the squash out on a baking sheet and roast for 1 hour, or until tender and lightly browned.

# BUFFALO PRIME RIB
# PARSLEY POPOVERS
# GRILLED ROSEMARY PEARS

 I didn't eat buffalo as a child, and the first time I tasted it I was reminded of the grass-fed beef I grew up with on my mom's ranch. It's lean yet tender, with hints of sweet grass and clover. It's best cooked to medium-rare. Here it's accompanied by eggy, light popovers to sop up the meat's delicious juices. The piney scent of rosemary nicely contrasts with the caramelized grilled pears. **SERVES 6**

## Buffalo Prime Rib

**1 large buffalo loin, about 4 pounds**

**Salt and freshly ground black pepper**

**1.** Preheat the oven to 350°F.

**2.** Season the buffalo with salt and pepper. Set the meat on a rack under a roasting pan and roast for 45 minutes, or until an instant-read thermometer reaches 120°F for very rare or 130°F for medium. Remove and allow to rest for 10 minutes before carving.

## Parsley Popovers

**1 tablespoon plus 1 teaspoon unsalted butter, melted**

**2 eggs**

**1 cup whole milk**

**½ teaspoon salt**

**1 cup all-purpose flour**

**2 tablespoons chopped fresh flat-leaf parsley**

**1.** Preheat the oven to 425°F.

**2.** Grease a 12-cup muffin or 6-cup popover tin with the 1 teaspoon melted butter and place in the oven while you prepare the batter.

(continues)

**3.** In a large bowl, beat together the eggs, milk, remaining 1 tablespoon butter, and the salt. Beat in the flour a little at a time until smooth. Fold in the parsley.

**4.** Fill the tins at least halfway full. Place in the oven and bake for 20 minutes, reduce the heat to 350°F, and continue baking for 15 to 25 minutes more, or until the popovers are puffed and browned. Serve immediately.

## Grilled Rosemary Pears

**6 Bosc pears**

**1 tablespoon chopped garlic**

**1 tablespoon chopped fresh rosemary**

**¼ cup olive oil**

**1.** Prepare a charcoal grill or preheat a gas grill to high.

**2.** Quarter and core the pears. Grill for 2 to 3 minutes on each side. Transfer the pears to a large bowl.

**3.** Gently toss with the garlic, rosemary, and oil to coat. Place back on the grill for 3 to 5 minutes.

# BUFFALO SHORT RIBS
## BARLEY RISOTTO
## STOUT-BRAISED PEARL ONIONS

 Be sure to use a cast-iron skillet to sear the ribs so they are crusty before adding the braising liquid. Meltingly tender, these short ribs in a cinnamon-spiked sauce are terrific on the creamy risotto. Pearl onions, braised in bitter stout, turn silky and fragrant to complete this lusty plate. **SERVES 6**

---

## Buffalo Short Ribs

2 cups all-purpose flour

Salt and freshly ground black pepper

5 pounds buffalo short ribs

2 tablespoons olive oil

½ cup chopped carrot

½ cup chopped onion

½ cup chopped celery

1 quart beef stock

2 bay leaves

2 sprigs fresh thyme

2 cinnamon sticks

2 tablespoons thyme leaves

**1.** Preheat the oven to 350°F.

**2.** Season the flour with salt and pepper. Spread the flour out on a plate and lightly coat the short ribs.

**3.** Heat the oil in a cast-iron skillet set over medium-high heat, and sear the ribs on all sides for 10 to 15 minutes, until caramel brown. Remove the ribs and set aside.

**4.** Add the carrot, onion, and celery to the pan and sauté for 5 to 8 minutes, until the vegetables are soft. Stir in the stock, scraping up the brown nubs clinging to the bottom of the pan.

**5.** Set the ribs in a roasting pan. Pour the vegetables and stock over the ribs; add the bay leaves, thyme, and cinnamon sticks.

**6.** Cover with plastic wrap, then with a layer of aluminum foil. Roast the ribs for 2½ to 3 hours, turning once each hour, until the meat is falling off the bones. Serve the ribs with the pan juices spooned over them, garnished with the thyme leaves.

GAME

# Barley Risotto

| 1 tablespoon unsalted butter | 4 quarts chicken stock, simmering | 3 tablespoons crème fraîche or sour cream |
| 1 white onion, chopped | 1 cup white wine | Salt and freshly ground black pepper |
| 1 cup pearl barley | | |

**1.** In a large saucepan set over low heat, melt the butter, add the onion, and sauté for 5 minutes, until translucent.

**2.** Add the barley and sauté, stirring, for 30 seconds to coat with the butter, then add 2 cups of the stock and bring to a boil. Reduce the heat and simmer, stirring, for 5 minutes, or until most of the stock is absorbed. Add the remaining stock, ½ cup at a time, allowing the stock to be absorbed before adding more and stirring frequently. Keep the barley covered when not stirring.

**3.** Add the wine ½ cup at a time, allowing it to be absorbed before adding more, stirring and cooking for 30 to 40 minutes, until the barley is tender.

**4.** Fold in the crème fraîche and season with salt and pepper.

# Stout-Braised Pearl Onions

| 1 tablespoon olive oil | 1½ cups stout beer | Salt and freshly ground black pepper |
| 2 pints (4 cups) pearl onions, peeled | 1 tablespoon unsalted butter | ½ teaspoon fresh thyme leaves |

**1.** In a deep saucepan set over medium heat, heat the oil and sauté the onions for 5 to 8 minutes, stirring so they brown on all sides.

**2.** Add the stout and cook for 15 minutes, or until it is reduced by half and the onions are tender.

**3.** Swirl in the butter and season with salt and pepper. Plate the onions and sauce with the meat. Garnish with the thyme leaves.

# BRAISED WILD BOAR SHANKS WITH APPLES
## POTATOES RACLETTE
# DIJON-CREAMED SPINACH

Wild boar, even those raised at game parks and on farms, roam outside, feasting on berries and nuts, so their meat is succulent and exceptionally flavorful. Take your time when searing these shanks so they develop a thick crust that will seal in the meat's juices and yield a rich, glossy sauce. These potatoes were inspired by raclette, a special dish from the Swiss Alps, where wild boar is prized. Just a dollop of Dijon mustard gives creamed spinach, that old favorite, a new spin. **SERVES 6**

## Braised Wild Boar Shanks with Apples

2 cups all-purpose flour

Salt and freshly ground black pepper

3 large boar shanks

2 tablespoons olive oil

½ cup chopped carrot

½ cup chopped onion

½ cup chopped celery

2 cups chicken stock

2 cups apple juice

2 bay leaves

2 sprigs fresh thyme

2 cinnamon sticks

1 star anise

3 whole cloves

2 Granny Smith apples, peeled, cored, and quartered

**1.** Preheat the oven to 350°F.

**2.** Season the flour with salt and pepper. Dust the boar with the seasoned flour and set aside.

**3.** Film a cast-iron skillet with the oil, set over medium-high heat, and sear the shanks on all sides for 10 to 15 minutes, working in batches so as not to crowd the pan. Remove the shanks and set aside.

**4.** Add the carrot, onion, and celery to the pan and sauté for 10 minutes, or until tender. Stir in the stock and apple juice, and scrape up any brown nubs on the bottom of the pan.

(continues)

**5.** Put the shanks in a roasting pan. Pour the vegetables with the stock and the apple juice over the shanks. Add the bay leaves, thyme, cinnamon sticks, star anise, cloves, and apples, and season with salt and pepper. Cover with plastic wrap and then with aluminum foil. Roast for 2 to 3 hours, turning every hour, until the meat is tender and falling off the bone.

**6.** Remove the meat and set aside. Strain the juices into a saucepan, removing the vegetables, herbs, and spices.

**7.** Set over high heat, bring to a boil, and reduce the liquid by half. Serve the shanks with the juices spooned on top.

## Potatoes Raclette

Salt

12 to 18 small Red Bliss potatoes

2 tablespoons unsalted butter

1 white onion, chopped

½ cup diced gherkins

1 cup grated Swiss cheese

**1.** Preheat the oven to 350°F.

**2.** Bring a large pot of lightly salted water to a boil over high heat. Cook the potatoes for 10 minutes, or until tender. Drain and transfer to a large bowl.

**3.** In a cast-iron skillet or large sauté pan, melt the butter and sauté the onion for 5 to 8 minutes, or until browned.

**4.** Stir in the potatoes and mash with a fork. Stir in the gherkins and top with the cheese.

**5.** Bake for 10 minutes, or until the cheese is bubbly.

# Dijon-Creamed Spinach

1 tablespoon unsalted butter

1½ pounds fresh spinach, stemmed and sliced into 2-inch strips

¼ cup heavy cream

¼ cup cream cheese

Pinch of grated nutmeg

1 tablespoon Dijon mustard

Salt and freshly ground black pepper

**1.** In a cast-iron skillet or large sauté pan, melt the butter over medium heat and cook the spinach for 2 minutes.

**2.** Stir in the cream, cream cheese, nutmeg, and mustard and simmer for 5 minutes. Season with salt and pepper.

TIP    In a pinch, substitute frozen spinach, but thaw and drain it thoroughly first.

# DUCK LEG TACOS
# WITH AVOCADO SALSA

This salsa is hot and creamy, the perfect match for rich, flavorful game. I like to use duck in this recipe, but leftover bison, venison, or antelope will work nicely, too. The heat from the jalapeño, which intensifies when chopped fine in a blender, is tamed by that classic cooling trio of cilantro, basil, and mint. **SERVES 6**

2 tablespoons fresh lime juice

2 ounces fresh basil

2 ounces fresh mint

2 ounces fresh cilantro

½ jalapeño, seeded and chopped, or more to taste

½ avocado, peeled and cubed

¼ cup olive oil

1 white onion, chopped

Salt and freshly ground black pepper

1 pound cooked duck leg meat, warmed

12 fresh corn or flour tortillas

½ cup diced radish

4 ounces queso fresco, crumbled

Lime wedges, for garnish

**1.** Put the lime juice, basil, mint, cilantro, jalapeño, avocado, and oil in a blender and process until smooth. Transfer to a small bowl and stir in the onion. Season with salt and pepper.

**2.** Shred the duck meat.

**3.** Toast the tortillas in a cast-iron skillet, plancha, or dry frying pan over medium-high heat.

**4.** Arrange equal portions of the duck on the tortillas, top with the salsa mixture, radish, and cheese, and serve immediately with the lime wedges for garnish.

# ONE-POT FAVORITES

It always feels good to create a dish that includes the delicious odds and ends of a previous dinner. These recipes are some of my favorites—humble and homey, easy to cook and serve—and most can be made ahead. Whether it's a hearty soup, stew, or casserole, my key to a great one-pot dinner is respect for each of the ingredients. Pay attention to colors and shapes. Vegetables should be cut the same size so they cook evenly. The meat pieces should be small enough to eat without cutting. These can be great for guests, too, requiring just a fork or spoon (no knife). Some of the one-pots need more time to cook than others, and everything isn't always tossed into the pot at once.

The recipes also make terrific leftovers and freeze well. Most double nicely, so make a few extra meals to freeze. You'll have dinner ready quickly on a busy night.

# SHEPHERD'S PIE CUPCAKES

This recipe is pure whimsy. Individual meatloaves are baked with a mashed potato topping. Kids (and people of all ages) will love these, especially if you use a pastry bag with a star tip to swirl the mashed potatoes on top. Don't hesitate to use leftover mashed potatoes from another dinner as the crust. **SERVES 6**

| | | |
|---|---|---|
| 1 tablespoon olive oil | 1 tablespoon chopped fresh sage | 4 russet potatoes, peeled and quartered |
| 2 pounds 80% to 90% lean ground beef | ¼ cup pine nuts, toasted | 1 teaspoon salt |
| 1 large shallot, chopped | 1 cup fresh bread crumbs | 2 egg yolks |
| | | 2 tablespoons whole milk |

**1.** Preheat the oven to 350°F.

**2.** Lightly grease 12 muffin cups with the oil.

**3.** In a large bowl, work together the ground beef, shallot, sage, pine nuts, and bread crumbs and set aside.

**4.** Put the potatoes in a large pot with enough water to cover and add the salt. Bring to a boil over high heat, then reduce the heat and simmer for 15 minutes, or until the potatoes are very tender.

**5.** Transfer the potatoes to a food processor or food mill and process until smooth. Put the whipped potatoes in a bowl and allow to cool a little.

**6.** Beat in the egg yolks one at a time, then beat in the milk.

**7.** Spoon the hamburger mixture into the muffin tins and bake for 30 minutes, or until the meat is cooked through (no longer pink).

**8.** Top with the mashed potatoes, then return to the oven and continue to bake for 10 to 15 minutes, until the potatoes are golden brown.

# RAHM'S CHILDHOOD CORN CHIP PIE

 *Everyone* will love this. It's terrific for tailgates, no matter where you're watching the game. Serve the meat right out of the cast-iron skillet. Growing up in Santa Fe, we used Fritos, but any favorite corn chip works well. You can make this extra-portable by using individual chip bags as serving cups. **SERVES 6**

2 pounds 80% lean ground beef

3 yellow onions, diced

½ cup all-purpose flour

½ cup spicy chili powder, or more to taste

1 teaspoon dried oregano

3 cups chicken stock

2 cups cooked pinto beans (see Note) or 1 16-ounce can, rinsed and drained

1 1-pound bag corn chips

1 cup shredded sharp Cheddar cheese

½ cup chopped fresh cilantro, for garnish

1 cup sour cream

**1.** Crumble the beef into a cast-iron skillet and set over medium-high heat.

**2.** Add 1 cup of the onions and cook, stirring, for 7 to 10 minutes, or until the beef is no longer pink and the onions are translucent.

**3.** Sprinkle in the flour, chili powder, and oregano and cook, stirring constantly for 2 to 3 minutes, until the flour turns dark brown and begins to form a thick, sticky layer on the bottom of the pan.

**4.** Stir in the stock, scraping up the dark, sticky layer, and bring to a simmer. Cook for 3 minutes, then stir in the pinto beans and the remaining onions. Continue cooking, uncovered, for 1 hour, or until the mixture is thick.

**5.** Pour the chips into 6 individual bowls. Spoon the beef and bean mixture over the top and then finish with the cheese. Garnish each bowl with the cilantro. Pass the sour cream on the side.

NOTE  To prepare pinto beans, rinse 1 cup of dried beans under cold water and discard any shriveled or black beans. Put the rinsed beans in a large saucepan or bowl, cover with water by 2 inches, and soak overnight.

# LAMB AND MUSHROOM STOUT POT PIE

 My version of the classic British meat pie calls for a good, strong stout—to cook with and to drink. This recipe also makes quick use of leftover beef, pork, lamb, or chicken from previous chapters. **SERVES 6**

**PASTRY**

1½ cups all-purpose flour, plus more for rolling the dough

½ teaspoon salt

½ cup (1 stick) unsalted butter

6 to 8 tablespoons ice water

**FILLING**

2 tablespoons unsalted butter

½ cup diced onion

½ cup diced celery

½ cup diced carrots

½ cup sliced mushrooms

2 pounds cooked lamb, cut into ½-inch dice

1 medium potato, peeled and cut into ½-inch dice

1 cup beef stock

½ cup stout beer

1 large rosemary sprig

**To make the pastry:**

**1.** Place the flour and salt in a food processor fitted with a steel blade and pulse to combine. Add the butter and pulse until the mixture resembles small peas.

**2.** Add 6 tablespoons of the ice water and pulse until the dough forms a ball, adding more water 1 tablespoon at a time if it seems too dry.

**3.** Cover with plastic wrap and refrigerate for at least 30 minutes (or overnight) before rolling it out.

**To make the filling:**

**1.** Set a cast-iron skillet or large sauté pan over medium-high heat. Melt 1 tablespoon of the butter and sauté the onion, celery, carrots, and mushrooms for 5 to 10 minutes, or until the vegetables release their juices and begin to brown.

**2.** Stir in the lamb and sauté for 5 minutes.

**3.** Stir in the potato, stock, and stout, scraping up any brown nubs that cling to the bottom of the pan. Add the rosemary, reduce the heat to a simmer, and cook for 10 minutes so the liquid is reduced to a thick sauce.

**4.** Preheat the oven to 425°F.

**To assemble:**

**1.** Place the filling in a deep 8-inch pie tin or casserole. Remove the rosemary. Dot the top with the remaining 1 tablespoon of butter.

**2.** Roll out the dough on a lightly floured board with a floured rolling pin and place it on top of the filling. Cut decorative slashes in the top of the dough.

**3.** Bake for 15 minutes, then reduce the temperature to 375°F and continue baking for 25 minutes, or until the crust is golden brown.

# GRILLED LAMB WITH PEACH BAGUETTE STUFFING

This dish is an easy, new take on lamb roulade. Instead of rolling the meat around the stuffing, a mix of peaches and crusty baguette tops grilled lamb for a carefree yet spectacular presentation. Ask the butcher to bone the roast so it's easy to flatten. **SERVES 6**

### GRILLED LEG OF LAMB

1 3½- to 4-pound leg of lamb, butterflied

1 tablespoon olive oil

Salt and freshly ground black pepper

### STUFFING

1 white onion, chopped

2 celery stalks, chopped

2 cups diced baguette

1 cup chicken stock

½ tablespoon chopped fresh sage

4 peaches, peeled and diced

**1.** To make the lamb: Cut the lamb in half and lay the 2 pieces between 2 sheets of parchment or wax paper. Using a meat mallet or a heavy pot, pound the meat to about ½ inch thick. Rub the lamb with the olive oil and sprinkle with salt and pepper. Preheat the oven to 350°F.

**2.** Set a cast-iron skillet over medium-high heat. Sear the lamb 3 minutes per side until nicely browned on both sides. Transfer the lamb to a baking sheet.

**3.** To make the stuffing: In a large saucepan, toss together the onion, celery, baguette, stock, and sage and cook for 3 minutes, or until the stock is fully absorbed.

**4.** Fold in the peaches and let stand at room temperature for 5 minutes.

**5.** To assemble: Preheat the oven to 350°F. Spread the peach crust over the lamb.

**6.** Bake for 15 to 20 minutes, until the crust is golden brown and the lamb has reached 125°F to135°F on an instant-read thermometer.

# PORK BELLY AND SHRIMP CASSOULET

 You can argue about what makes a genuine "cassoulet," but really, it's just a baked dish of sausage and beans. Warming and hearty, this is one of those dishes that tastes even better served the next day. **SERVES 6**

1 pound pork belly, cut into 1-inch pieces

1 white onion, chopped

1 cup chicken stock

1 cup white wine

1 bay leaf

½ pound large shrimp, cleaned and deveined

1 large cauliflower, broken into florets

1 cup cooked or canned white beans, drained

½ cup diced roasted red peppers (see page 183)

1 lemon, cut into 6 wedges, for garnish

**1.** Preheat the oven to 350°F.

**2.** In a Dutch oven set over medium-high heat, cook the pork belly and onion for 5 to 10 minutes, until the fat is rendered and the onion is soft. Stir in the stock and wine and scrape up any nubs that cling to the bottom of the pot.

**3.** Turn the pork mixture and liquid into a casserole or large ovenproof pot. Add the bay leaf, shrimp, cauliflower, beans, and peppers. Bake for 30 minutes, stirring halfway through, or until the shrimp curl and turn pink and the top is crusty.

**4.** Remove the bay leaf and serve with a wedge of lemon on the side.

# LAMB MERGUEZ–LENTIL STEW

Lamb Merguez, or Spanish sausages, are laced with harissa, fennel, and garlic to give this simple stew its bold flavors. I like to soak the lentils a day ahead so they open fully without any hard covering as they cook. They thicken this stew without the addition of a roux, so though it's hearty, it's also light and relatively healthy. Make it ahead; it tastes even better the next day. **SERVES 6**

| | | |
|---|---|---|
| 6 ounces dried lentils | 1 medium onion, diced | 1 bay leaf |
| 2 tablespoons olive oil | 1 fennel bulb, diced | 2 sprigs fresh thyme |
| 1 pound Merguez sausages, cut into 2-inch rounds | 2 medium carrots, diced | |
| | 1 quart chicken stock | |

**1.** One day before preparing this recipe, soak the lentils in water to cover by 2 inches. Drain and set aside.

**2.** In a large, deep saucepan set over medium heat, add the oil and sauté the sausages, onion, fennel, and carrots for 5 to 10 minutes, until the sausage has rendered its fat and the vegetables are very tender.

**3.** Stir in the stock, lentils, bay leaf, and thyme. Reduce the heat so the liquid simmers, cover, and cook for 1 hour. Remove and discard the bay leaf and thyme.

**4.** Remove 1 cup of the lentils and vegetables, being careful not to pick up any of the sausage, and puree in a blender until smooth. Return to the pot, stir, and serve.

> **TIP** This recipe doubles nicely. Make an extra batch and allow it to cool. Then package it in quart-size freezer containers. Store in the freezer for up to 6 months.

MEAT AND POTATOES

222

# GRILLED CURRY CHICKEN WITH SWEET POTATOES AND PEAS

This is a recipe I perfected while living on St. Lucia, a romantic hideaway in the Caribbean, while opening three new restaurants for Rock Resorts. I reached out to local cooks to learn about their native dishes prepared over open fires. Grilling chicken first adds a smoky note to the stew's sun-kissed spices. The potatoes melt as they cook in the pot and thicken the broth, eliminating the need for flour or cornstarch. Serve the chicken wrapped in a roti, an Indian tortilla, and you'll have a casual handheld meal. **SERVES 6**

2 whole skin-on boneless chicken breasts, 2 pounds each

2 russet potatoes, peeled and cut into 2-inch cubes

1 small sweet potato, peeled and cut into 2-inch cubes

2 small white onions, cut into 2-inch cubes

2 garlic cloves, peeled

2 tablespoons curry powder

1½ cups chicken stock

½ cup fresh or frozen peas

1 14-ounce can coconut milk

Salt and freshly ground black pepper

¼ cup chopped fresh cilantro

**1.** Prepare a charcoal grill or preheat a gas grill to high.

**2.** Grill the chicken breasts for 4 to 5 minutes, then flip and continue grilling for 4 to 5 minutes, or until golden brown and lightly charred. Remove and allow to cool. Cut the chicken into 2-inch pieces.

**3.** Put the chicken, potatoes, sweet potato, onions, garlic, curry powder, and stock in a large deep saucepan and set over medium-high heat. Bring to a boil, then reduce the heat to a simmer, cover, and cook for 15 minutes, or until the potatoes are soft. Add the peas and simmer for another 3 to 5 minutes, until the peas are bright green and cooked through.

**4.** Stir in the coconut milk. Season with salt and pepper. Fold in the cilantro right before serving.

# ROTISSERIE CHICKEN NOODLE SOUP

Rotisserie chicken makes terrific soup. The nicely browned chicken gives the stock a deep roasted flavor and the meal comes together in a wink. Use hunks of zesty, cheesy cornbread to mop up every last drop from your bowl. **SERVES 6**

1 rotisserie chicken

2 tablespoons unsalted butter

1 celery stalk, chopped

1 white onion, chopped

1 tablespoon chopped fresh flat-leaf parsley

1 bay leaf

1 quart chicken stock

4 ounces spaghetti, broken

1 teaspoon truffle oil, optional

**1.** Remove the meat from the chicken and discard the bones and skin.

**2.** In a large soup pot set over medium-high heat, melt the butter and sauté the celery and onion for 5 minutes, or until soft. Stir in the parsley, bay leaf, and stock and bring to a boil.

**3.** Add the spaghetti and cook for 10 to 12 minutes, until al dente. Reduce the heat, stir in the chicken, and heat through. Stir in the truffle oil if you wish.

# SPICY ITALIAN SAUSAGE STEW

This stew is terrific and remarkably easy to make. It's delicious served with crusty bread to wipe up the sauce left on your plate. It is the perfect winter dish to make a day ahead and bring to a potluck. When it sits overnight, the flavors have a chance to marry, so don't hesitate to make it ahead. **SERVES 6**

---

2 pounds bulk Italian sausage

1 white onion, chopped

1 cup chicken stock

1 pound cremini mushrooms, sliced

1 pound baby red potatoes, sliced

1 cup canned diced tomatoes with juice

1 large fennel bulb, sliced

2 sprigs fresh rosemary

1 teaspoon red pepper flakes, or to taste

1 whole head of garlic, top and loose outer papery skins removed

**1.** In a cast-iron skillet or large sauté pan set over medium-high heat, cook the sausage and onion for 5 to 10 minutes, stirring and crumbling the sausage until it's no longer pink and the onion is tender.

**2.** Stir in the stock, mushrooms, potatoes, tomatoes with their juices, fennel, rosemary, red pepper flakes, and garlic. Reduce the heat and simmer, uncovered, for 10 to 15 minutes, or until the potatoes are tender and the liquid is thick.

**3.** Remove the rosemary and garlic before serving.

> TIP  This stew freezes nicely. Store it in either individual-size or large containers.

# PAELLA WITH PEPPER BACON

Among the many variations on the classic Spanish recipe for paella, this is one of the easiest and most straightforward. Don't be put off by the long list of ingredients—it comes together in a snap. And don't hesitate to vary them to suit your tastes. Try thinly sliced spicy Spanish chorizo sausages instead of the bacon, add chopped lobster tails along with the scallops and shrimp. This classic stew of chicken and seafood is great for a big party. Be sure to serve it with thick slices of crusty bread to sop up the juices. **SERVES 6**

6 skin-on chicken thighs, 1½ to 1¾ pounds

Salt and freshly ground black pepper

1 tablespoon olive oil

12 ounces country-style pepper bacon, cut into ½-inch dice

1 white onion, diced

3 garlic cloves, crushed

Pinch of red pepper flakes

1 cup long-grain rice

2 tablespoons tomato paste

2 cups chicken stock

1 cup clam juice

1 4-ounce can roasted red peppers, drained

1 teaspoon saffron threads

1 bay leaf

4 sprigs fresh thyme

6 ounces shrimp, cleaned and deveined

6 to 12 fresh clams, in their shells

6 ounces bay scallops

½ cup fresh or frozen peas

2 tablespoons chopped fresh flat-leaf parsley, for garnish

**1.** Preheat the oven to 350°F.

**2.** Season the chicken with salt and pepper. In a cast-iron skillet or large, deep ovenproof sauté or paella pan, heat the oil and sauté the chicken for 3 to 5 minutes on each side, or until lightly browned. Remove and set aside.

**3.** Add the bacon and cook, stirring, for 3 to 5 minutes, or until the fat is rendered and the bacon begins to crisp. Remove and set aside with the chicken.

**4.** Add the onion, garlic, red pepper flakes, rice, and tomato paste and sauté for 2 or 3 minutes, stirring, until the rice is coated with the tomato paste and becomes brown and sticky. Stir in the stock and clam juice, scraping up any brown nubs from the bottom of the pan, then add the peppers, saffron, bay leaf, and thyme and bring to a boil over high heat. Reduce the heat and simmer, stirring occasionally, for 10 minutes.

**5.** Add the shrimp, clams, and scallops and return the chicken and bacon to the pan. Cover and cook for 5 minutes, or until the clams open and the shrimp turn pink. Stir in the peas.

**6.** Roast the paella in the oven for 10 minutes, so the sides and top become crusty. Remove the bay leaf and thyme sprigs. Serve garnished with the parsley.

# SOURCES & RESOURCES

## BEEF

**DANCING FORKS MEAT COMPANY**
Dancing Forks has been providing the highest quality premium steaks and chops to restaurants for over fifty years and is a great source for home cooks seeking steakhouse-quality beef. DancingForksMeatCompany.com; 949-415-6328.

## LAMB, GAME, AND SPECIALTY POULTRY

**PRAIRIE HARVEST SPECIALTY FOOD**
For more than thirty years, Prairie Harvest has been providing chefs and home cooks with premium lamb and game, including buffalo, venison, and elk. Working with a variety of ranchers who manage land using best conservation practices, Prairie Harvest is helping to maintain our country's natural resources while providing great food. PrairieHarvest.com; 800-350-7166.

## COOKING SCHOOLS

**THE SANTA FE SCHOOL OF COOKING & MARKET**
The Santa Fe School of Cooking specializes in teaching foods of the Southwest. The adjacent market is filled with New Mexican food products and cookware, and they ship across the country. SanteFeSchoolOfCooking.com; 800-982-4688.

# ACKNOWLEDGMENTS

Mary Fama—It all started with you and those Bologna mountains. Your love and encouragement keep me going every day. Without you, I never would have found the drive to make better food. Celso and Rose, I know you are looking down from heaven and watching over me. Celso, you taught me the value of hard work; Rose, you just told me *"comer comer,"* eat eat.

Delani, Kalli, and Reese Fama—You are my inspiration, my dreams, my future. Kerri, Jim, and Cindy, thanks so much for being there through this long career. Our kids are amazing because of you.

Aunt Joanna and Bill—You believed in me, took me in, and gave me my first taste of cooking. I'm not yet full. You showed me that everything in life should be an adventure. To my large and wonderful family, thank you for cheering me on!

Robin Kuzma—You are the reason I stayed in L.A. and kept the dream alive. Thank you for tasting and testing my recipes, and for joining me in this adventure.

Charmaine, Cliff, and Dakota—Thank you for your encouragement and love early in my life.

Vanessa, Art, and Pops (my big dawg!)—Thanks for your talent and inspiration.

Vazquez Family—Thanks for teaching me style and grace, how to work hard, play hard, and never stop.

Angela Payton—Your wine palate is amazing; your tech skills are brilliant. Thanks for keeping me on track.

Alessandro Stratta—Thanks for making the art of cooking so damn cool and for hiring me for my first real cooking job. I've come a long way.

Chef Jim Cohen—You were a true mentor. Thanks for treating me like a big dog. I will never forget this Jim Brown quote: "Attitude is everything, and no one blocked for me."

Kevin Gay—You truly taught me everything about cooking. To this day you are still making the best gnocchi I've ever tasted.

Jeffrey Russell—Thanks for the tough love and for teaching me that fine-dining food can never be too fancy.

Chef Sigfried Eisenberber, Robert Huckles, and Steven Bartolin—Thanks for teaching me how to do it right in mass quantities and for giving me a chance to play in the kitchen.

Serge Raoul and Cindy Smith—Thanks for giving me an enviable opportunity in your beautiful hotel in New Mexico and for introducing me to the wonderful city of New York. You are great spiritual guides and amazing restaurateurs.

Michael McPhie—You are a fantastic F&B director. You gave me freedom to source and work with the best and most exciting ingredients in the world.

Matthew Merrill—Thanks for being a great friend, an amazing server, and my biggest fan.

Thanks to Tyler Delaney and Westport Entertainment for all the hard work and support. This book was very much on my bucket list, and you made it happen.

Beth Dooley—What a terrific partner you've been, getting my ideas, recipes, and story down on the page.

Emily Takoudes—I couldn't have asked for a more patient and knowledgeable editor. Thanks so much for your vision and guidance.

Jennifer May—Thank you so much for your spectacular photography.

Jane Treuhaft, art director; Ashley Tucker, designer; Terry Deal, production editor; Jessica Freeman-Slade, assistant editor; and the whole team at Clarkson Potter—Thanks to each of you for your talents in creating a beautiful book.

Santa Fe, dear Santa Fe—Thank you for being such a great food town to grow up in. Thanks to Coyote Café for not firing me and instead throwing me into the kitchen. That's where it all began . . .

# INDEX